Anonymous

Statement of the Disposition of Some of the Bodies of Deceased Union Soldiers

and prisoners of war whose remains have been removed to national cemeteries in the southern and western states

Anonymous

Statement of the Disposition of Some of the Bodies of Deceased Union Soldiers
and prisoners of war whose remains have been removed to national cemeteries in the southern and western states

ISBN/EAN: 9783744793971

Printed in Europe, USA, Canada, Australia, Japan

Cover: Foto ©ninafisch / pixelio.de

More available books at **www.hansebooks.com**

STATEMENT

OF THE

DISPOSITION OF SOME OF THE BODIES

OF

DECEASED UNION SOLDIERS

AND

PRISONERS OF WAR

WHOSE REMAINS HAVE BEEN REMOVED

TO

NATIONAL CEMETERIES

IN THE SOUTHERN AND WESTERN STATES.

VOLUME I.

"True to their Country and God,
To meet at the last reveillé."

WASHINGTON:
GOVERNMENT PRINTING OFFICE.
1868.

STATEMENT OF FINAL DISPOSITION, VOL. I.

GENERAL ORDERS }   QUARTERMASTER GENERAL'S OFFICE,
No. 8.   }   WASHINGTON, D. C., *February* 24, 1868.

The following statement of the disposition of some of the bodies of deceased Union Soldiers and Prisoners of War whose remains have been removed to National Cemeteries in the Southern and Western States, prepared in this Office under the direction of Brevet Brigadier General A. J. PERRY, Q. M., U. S. Army, is published by authority of the Secretary of War, for the information of surviving comrades and friends, and for use in connection with the "Rolls of Honor" heretofore published by this Office.

D. H. RUCKER,
Acting Quartermaster General,
Brevet Major General, U. S. A.

QUARTERMASTER GENERAL'S OFFICE,
WASHINGTON, D. C., *February* 8, 1868.

Brevet Major General D. H. RUCKER,
Acting Quartermaster General,
U. S. Army,

GENERAL:

The enclosed "Statement of the *Final Disposition* of the Bodies of Deceased Union Soldiers and Prisoners of War, whose remains have been removed to National Cemeteries in the Southern and Western States," prepared in this Office by Brevet Colonel C. W. FOLSOM, A. Q. M., U. S. Vols., is respectfully transmitted to you, with the request that it be printed and distributed for use in connection with the "Rolls of Honor" heretofore issued from this Office.

I am, General, very respectfully,
Your obedient servant,

ALEX. J. PERRY,
Bv't Brig. General and Q. M., U. S. A.

QUARTERMASTER GENERAL'S OFFICE,
DIVISION OF CEMETERIES,
WASHINGTON, D. C., *February* 7, 1868.

Brevet Brig. General A. J. PERRY,
    Quartermaster, U. S. Army,
  Q. M. General's Office, Washington, D. C.,

GENERAL:

I have the honor to transmit herewith for publication, as a companion volume to the "Rolls of Honor" now being published by this Office, a Statement of the *Final Disposition* of some of the Bodies of Deceased Union Soldiers and Prisoners of War whose remains have been removed to the various National Cemeteries in the Southern and Western States.

Owing to the vast field of operations of the Armies of the United States during the war, it has been found that the collection and the removal of the bodies of the dead has been a much slower and more laborious task than was at first supposed.

Thus, the within statement (which only embraces a portion of such removals) shows that 47,368 bodies of deceased Union Soldiers and Prisoners of War have been removed from 237 different localities, scattered throughout the Southern and Western States, to 30 of the established National Cemeteries, where their remains now rest, side by side, under the perpetual care and protection of the Government for the defense of which they sacrificed their lives.

It is thought that this statement will furnish valuable materials for future records, and some assistance in identifying the great number of those whose graves now bear only the sad inscription: "Unknown U. S. Soldier."

Similar statements will be prepared, from time to time, as the necessary information is received in this Office, thus finally furnishing a complete record of all such removals of the remains of deceased Union Soldiers.

    I am, General, very respectfully,
        Your obedient servant,

            C. W. FOLSOM,
           Bvt. Colonel and A. Q. M. Vols.

TABLE OF CONTENTS.

States from and to which the Bodies of Deceased Union Soldiers and Prisoners of War have been removed.

Number.	From places in—	To Cemeteries in—	Page.
I.	Maryland, Virginia, and the District of Columbia.	Virginia	8
II.	Virginia	Virginia	8–16
III.	North Carolina	North Carolina	16–17
IV.	Georgia	Georgia	18
V.	Louisiana and Mississippi	Louisiana	19–21
VI.	Texas	Texas	21
VII.	Tennessee, Alabama, Georgia, and Virginia.	Tennessee	22–23
VIII.	Illinois, Kentucky, and Missouri	Illinois	24
IX.	Missouri	Missouri	25–26
X.	Colorado Territory	Colorado Territory	26
	Alphabetical Index of places from which bodies have been removed		27–28
	Alphabetical Index of Cemeteries to which bodies have been removed		29

I.—From Maryland, Virginia, and the District of Columbia, to Virginia.

No.	Number and Original Location of Graves.		Date of Removal of Bodies.	Final Disposition of Remains.		Remarks.
	Number of Graves.	Original Location.		Number of Bodies.	Final Resting-place.	
1						
2	292	Montgomery county, Md.				
3	22	Prince George's county, Md.				
4	61	District of Columbia.	Oct. 23, 1865, to July 31, 1866.	4,368	Arlington National Cemetery, Va., (District of Columbia.)	
5	843	Fairfax county, Va.				
6	618	Alexandria county, Va.				
7	98	Loudon county, Va.				
8	1,791	Bull Run Battle-fields, Fairfax county, Va.	June & July, '66.			
9	643	On line of Orange and Alex'a R. R., bet. Alex'a and Rappahannock Crossing, Va.	May 17, 1866, to Sept. 9, 1866.			
10						
11	1,245	Culpeper county, Orange C. H., and Gordonsville, Va.	July 11, 1866, to Mar. 31, 1867.	1,245	Culpeper National Cemetery, (at Culpeper C. H.,) Va.	
12	2	Mr. Gatewood's Farm, Va.				
13	3	" Tait's "				
14	16	" Atkins' "				
15	1	" Kemp's "				
16	9	" Brackett's "	Kent, and Charles City, Va.			
17	4	" Benford's "				
18	5	" Johnson's "				
19	1	" Hare's "				
20	5	" Ampler's "				
21	2	" Brightel's "				
22	4	" Warner's "				
23	2	" Woodpark's "				
24	299	" Frayser's "				
25	108	" Robertson's "				
26	1	" Biddle's "				
27	9	" Daggett's "				
28	4	" Whitlock's "				
29	2	" Turpin's "				

30	Mr.	Nelson's	Farm, Va.	46	May 7, 1866, to July 14, 1866.
31	"	Christian's	" "	9	
32	"	Fisher's	" "	6	
33	"	Ladd's	" "	11	
34	"	Mountcassel's	" "	9	
35	"	Walter's	" "	9	
36	"	Colgan's	" "	6	
37	"	Maddox's	" "	1	1,197
38	"	Hobson's	" "	1	Glendale National Cemetery, Virginia, (about 10 miles S. E. of Richmond, on Nelson's Farm, Charles City county, Va.)
39	"	Pierman's	" "	6	
40	"	Nance's	" "	1	
41	"	Masten's	" "	3	
42	"	Jordan's	" "	4	
43	"	Crump's	" "	3	
44	"	Hubbard's	" "	3	
45	"	O'Day's	" "	5	
46	"	McDowell's	" "	4	
47	"	Harrison's Landing, Va.		314	
48	"	Fussell's Mill, (near Richmond, Va.)		100	
49	"	Malvern Hill,	" "	209	
50	"	Salem Church,	" "	3	
51	"	Samaria Church,	" "	4	
52	"	Wilson's Landing,	" "	33	
		Total removed to Glendale		1,197	

II.—From places in Virginia to Virginia.

53	Mr.	Childrey's Farm, Va.		79	May 10, 1866, to July 14, 1866.
54	"	Aiken's	" "	126	
55	"	Allen's	" "	28	
56	"	Bottom's	" "	2	
57	"	Robinson's	" "	1	
58	"	Sweeney's	" "	4	309
59	"	Chapin's	" "	3	Fort Harrison National Cemetery, Va., on Molly Burdon's Farm, (Henrico county, Va.)
60	"	Adcock's	" "	11	
61	"	Burdon's	" "	15	
62	"	Alter's	" "	11	
63	"	Cox's	" "	11	
64	"	James'	" "	7	
65	"	Stearnes'	" "	11	
		Carried forward		309	

From *Virginia* to *Virginia*—Continued.

No.	Number and Original Location of Graves.		Date of Removal of Bodies.	Final Disposition of Remains.		Remarks.
	Number of Graves.	Original Location.		Number of Bodies.	Final Resting-place.	
		Brought forward		309		
66	11	Mr. McCoull's Farm, Va.				
67	5	Mr. Yarborough's Farm, Va.				
68	9	Mayor Allen's "				
69	3	Colonel Knight's "				
70	11	Mr. Dayhart's "				
71	17	" Hutchinson's "				
72	101	" Gatbright's "				
73	3	" Pierce's "				
74	6	" Throckmorton's "	In the counties of Henrico and Chesterfield, Virginia.			
75	8	" Gerhart's "				
76	5	" Darby's "				
77	1	" Johnson's "				
78	1	" Bailey's "		505	Fort Harrison National Cemetery, Va., on Molly Burdon's Farm, (Henrico county, Va.)	
79	1	" Jordan's "	May 10, 1866, to July 14, 1866.			
80	1	" Martin's "				
81	4	" Clark's "				
82	2	" Buffin's "				
83	1	" Bowler's "				
84	4	" Roper's "				
85	112	Deep Bottom, (10 miles S. E. of Rich'd, Va.,) "				
86	25	Dutch Gap, (10 miles S. E. of Rich'd,) "				
87	2	Fort Johnson, "				
88	110	Fort Gilman, "				
89	18	Fort Harrison, "				
90	1	Laurel Hill, (near Richmond,) "				
91	38	Fussell's Mill, (near Richmond,) "				
92	5	Mr. Burdon's Farm, "				
		Total removed to Fort Harrison		814		

93	Mr. E. D. Wade's Farm, Va.	24		
94	" Tucker's "	5		
95	" Barnett's "	169		
96	" Golding's "	1		
97	" Kelley's "	48		
98	" Paaley's "	1		
99	" Newton's "	37		
100	" Slaughter's "	100		
101	" Johnson's "	21		
102	" Bayley's "	8		
103	Mrs. Rachel Ball's "	3		
104	Mr. Alexander's "	1		In the counties of Hanover, King William, and Henrico, Va.
105	Mr. Baskett's "	51		
106	Mrs. Bowles' "	70		
107	Mr. Jenkins' "	6		
108	Col. Richardson's "	16		
109	Mr. Martin's "	54		
110	" Gathright's "	318		
111	" Wood's "	8		
112	" White's "	9	Feb. 27, 1866, to Mar. 30, 1866.	
113	" L. King's "	15		
114	" Bosher's "	50		
115	" McGhee's "	289	1,781	Cold Harbor National Cemetery, Va., (10 miles north of Richmond,) on Miss Indiana Slaughter's Farm, Hanover county, Va.
116	" Stewart's "	5		
117	" Wright's "	1		
118	" J. Baskin's "	4		
119	" Wm. Gaines' "	34		
120	" Woodey's "	38		
121	" Boze's "	7		
122	" Higgin's "	1		
123	" Buffin's "	2		
124	" Ashlee's "	4		
125	Dr. Tyler's "	24		
126	Mr. Turner's "	3		
127	" John Codom's "	2		
128	6th Corps Hospital, "	151		
129	18th Corps Hospital, "	190		
130	{ Bethesda Church, (10 miles north of Richmond, Va.) }	11		
	Carried forward			1,781

From Virginia to Virginia—Continued.

No.	Number and Original Location of Graves.		Date of Removal of Bodies.	Final Disposition of Remains.		Remarks.
	Number of Graves.	Original Location.		Number of Bodies.	Final Resting-place.	
131	92	Brought forward	} Feb. 27, 1866, to Mar. 30, 1866. In the counties of Hanover, K. William, & Hen'o, Va.	1,781	Cold Harbor National Cemetery, Va., (10 miles north of Richmond,) on Miss Indiana Slaughter's Farm, Hanover county, Va.	
132	55	Cold Harbor, (10 miles north of Richmond, Va.)				
133	2	Hanover C. H., Va.		149		
		Hall's Shop, "				
		Total removed to Cold Harbor		1,930		
134	65	Mrs. Allen's Farm, Va.			} Charles City, Va.	
135	59	Mr. Gatewood's Farm, Va.				
136	76	" Adams' "				
137	3	" Jurton's "				
138	1	" Sharp's "				
139	6	" Golden's "				
140	60	" Hayes' "				
141	33	" Bragg's "				
142	4	" Williams' "				
143	22	" Trent's "				
144	42	" Tignor's "				
145	8	" Coombs' "				
146	1	" Gartner's "				
147	50	" Baxter's "				
148	67	" Hillard's "				
149	56	" Hitchcock's "				
150	18	" Leber's "				
151	18	" Royster's "				
152	67	" Turner's "				
153	1	" Carter's "				
154	6	" Wade's "				
155	18	" Bridgewater's "				

156	Mr. Vaughn's Farm, Va.	2		
157	" Camden's "	1		
158	" Hicks' "	37		
159	" Echo's "	52		
160	" Keaslowe's "	5		
161	" Whiteside's "	2		
162	" Chas. Martin's "	3		
163	" Mathew's "	3		
164	" Sidney's "	2		
165	" Ryan's "	6		
166	" J. Sherman's "	5		
167	" Hughes' "	3		
168	" R. T. Graves' "	1	In the counties of Henrico, New Kent, and May 1, 1866, to June 27, 1866.	1,339 Seven Pines National Cemetery, Va., (about 10 miles S. E. of Richmond,) on Chas. Hilliard's Farm, Henrico county, Va.
169	" White's "	4		
170	" Courtney's "	2		
171	" Foster's "	43		
172	" Field's "	5		
173	" Gathright's "	3		
174	" Taylor's "	11		
175	Mrs. Morgan's "	2		
176	Mr. Parr's "	1		
177	" Michie's "	9		
178	" Jos. Allen's "	2		
179	" Gaines' "	3		
180	" Fitzwilson's "	16		
181	" King's "	9		
182	" Garnett's "	42		
183	" Watt's "	1		
184	" White's "	3		
185	" Bottom's "	2		
186	" B. Martin's "	3		
187	" Anderson's "	11		
188	" Quall's "	17		
189	" Acree's "	28		
190	" Kuhr's "	9		
191	" Watkin's "	31		
192	Mount Castle	4		
193	Fair Oaks, (8 miles N. E. of Richmond,) Va.	269		
194	Savage Station, Va.			
	Carried forward			1,338

From Virginia to Virginia—Continued.

No.	Number and Original Location of Graves.		Date of Removal of Bodies.	Final Disposition of Remains.		Remarks.
	Number of Graves.	Original Location.		Number of Bodies.	Final Resting-place.	
		Brought forward............		1,338		
195	3	Chestnut Grove Church, Va...	May 1, 1866, to June 27, 1866. In the counties of Henrico, N. Kent, & Charles City, Va.	18	Seven Pines National Cemetery, Va, (about 10 miles S. E. of Richmond,) on Chas. Hilliard's Farm, Henrico county, Va.	
196	11	Antioch Church, "				
197	1	Summit Station, "				
198	3	Meadow Station, (5 miles N. of Rich'd,) Va.				
		Total removed to Seven Pines......		1,356		
199	440	White House Landing, (on York River,) Va.	York, and Elizabeth City, Va.			
200	1	New Point Light-house, "				
201	8	Brighton, "				
202	1	Fort at Yorktown, "				
203	4	King and Queen's Court-house, "				
204	4	Cumberland, (25 miles N. E. of Rich'd) "				
205	42	Mechanicsville, (5 miles N. of Rich'd,) "				
206	3	Yorktown Post, (York county,) "				
207	1	King William's Court-house, "				
208	41	Enoch Church, "				
209	3	Dicord Bridge, "				
210	2	Cheeseman's Landing, "				
211	4	Crump's X Roads, "				
212	4	Williamsburg, "				
213	13	Carr's Church, "				
214	15	Young's Mills, (Warwick county,) "				
215	4	Grafton Church, "				
216	4	William's Ferry, (York county,) "				
217	32	Brick House Point, (New Kent county,) "				

No.	Location		State	Date	Total	Cemetery
218	30	Ship Point, (York county,)	Va.	July 13, 1866, to Feb. 23, 1867.	1,497	Yorktown National Cemetery, Virginia, (York county, Va.)
219	5	Zion Church,	"			
220	2	Olive Branch,	"			
221	14	West Point, (King William's county,)	"			
222	3	Yorktown Beach, (York county,)	"			
223	15	Upper Grafton Church,	"			
224	4	Warwick Court-house,	"			
225	2	Mr. J. Wood's Farm,	"			
226	64	" Wm. Allen's "	"			
227	39	" Dobson's "	"			
228	2	" Buck's "	"			
229	19	" Lumberlick's "	"			
230	2	Mrs. Hayne's "	"			
231	1	Dr. Jones' "	"			
232	16	Mr. Haws' "	"			
233	34	" Haze's "	"			
234	4	" Payne's "	"			
235	44	" Cook's "	"			
236	5	" Lerrel's "	"			
237	51	" Clark's "	"			
238	1	" Walker's "	"			
239	291	" R. P. Waller's Farm,	"			
240	45	" Hogg's "	"			
241	19	" Whitaker's "	"			
242	44	Dr. Morris' "	"			
243	29	" Powers' "	"			
244	1	Capt. Crockett's "	"			
245	2	Mr. Finlick's "	"			
246	5	" Wm. Lively's "	"			
247	8	" Anderson's "	"			
248	23	" Robert Sander's "	"			
249	1	" Thos. Edwards' "	"			
250	2	" Wm. Garrow's "	"			
251	10	" Whilback's "	"			
252	1	" James Green's "	"			
253	23	" White's "	"			
254	1	" E. Tab's "	"			
255	1	" J. Patrick's "	"			
256	8	" Wynn's "	"			

In the counties of Gloucester, Warwick.

Carried forward............ 1,497

16

From Virginia to Virginia—Continued.

No.	Number and Original Location of Graves.		Date of Removal of Bodies.	Final Disposition of Remains.		Remarks.
	Number of Graves.	Original Location.		Number of Bodies.	Final Resting-place.	
		Brought forward.........		1,497		
257	1	Mrs. Clarke's Farm, Va.........	} July 13, 1866, to Feb. 13, 1867. In the counties of York, Gloucester, Warwick, & Elizabeth City, Va.	} 683	} Yorktown National Cemetery, Virginia, (York county, Va.)	
258	1	Pippintree Ferry, (20 miles N. E. of Richmond,) Va.........				
259	636	Original Cemetery, Yorktown, Va.........				
260	45	Mrs. Carter's Farm, Va.........				
		Total removed to Yorktown.........		2,180		
		Removed to Cemeteries in Virginia.........		{ 4,368 1,245 1,197 814 1,930 1,356 2,180	Arlington. Culpeper. Glendale. Fort Harrison. Cold Harbor. Seven Pines. Yorktown.	
		Total.........		13,090		

III.—From places in North Carolina to North Carolina.

261	1	Neuse River Road, (4 miles from Raleigh,) North Carolina.........				
262	1	Neuse River Road, (7 miles from Raleigh, under a shelving rock about 250 yards from road and 150 yards from house owned by the late J. Mordecai, esq.,) N. C.				
263	1	City Cemetery, Goldsboro', N. C.........				
264	4	City Cemetery, Raleigh, N. C.........				

No.	Number	Location	Date	Cemetery
265	1	Wellsboro' Road, (3 miles from Raleigh and 125 yards from road, on land called Wilder's Tract,) N. C.		
266	1	Brown's land, (3 miles from Raleigh, on Hillsboro' Road,) N. C.		
267	1	Frank Page's land, (500 yards southwest of Haywood's Road,) N. C.		
268	4	Raleigh Small-pox burying ground, (¼ mile north of Raleigh,) N. C.	Aug. 1, 1867, to Aug. 14, 1867.	Raleigh National Cemetery, N. C., (Wake county, N. C.) 963
269	1	D. Lein's land, (plantation 10 miles from Raleigh,) N. C.		
270	1	Holleman's Road, (1¼ mile from Raleigh,) N. C.		
271	3	Fayetteville Road, (10 miles from Raleigh,) N. C.		
272	2	Hillsboro' Road, (¼ mile south of road, and 3 miles from Raleigh,) N. C.		
273	280	Goldsboro',	Feb. 18 to 20, '67.	
274	2	Smithfield,	Feb. 21, 1867	
275	73	Greensboro'	Feb. 27, 1867	
276	487	Raleigh,	Feb. 20 to 24, '67.	
277	1,066	Newbern, (Stanley Cemetery,)	Do	
278	145	Newbern, (Cedar Grove Cem'y,)	Do	Newbern National Cemetery, N. C., (Jones county, N. C.) 1,793
279	59	Bachelor's Creek,	Do	
280	221	Beaufort,	March, 1867	
281	223	Morehead City,	Do	
282	79	Battle-field, (5 miles from Newbern,) N. C.	Do	
283	781	Fort Fisher, "	Do	
284	73	Brunswick, "	Do	
285	21	Hilton, "	Do	
286	128	Kidder & Martin's Mills, (Wilmington,) "	Do	Wilmington National Cemetery, N. C., on J. D. Rytenberg's Farm, (Brunswick county, N. C.) 1,699
287	149	Marine Hospital, (Wilmington,) "	Do	
288	12	Baptist Church, (Wilmington,) "	Do	
289	22	Cone Cemetery, (Wilmington,) "	Do	
290	410	Oakdale Cemetery, (Wilmington,) "	Do	
291	10	North East, "	Do	
292	93	Smithville, "	Do	
293	19	Fayetteville, N. C.	Do	19

Total removed to Cemeteries in N. C. 4,374

IV.—From places in Georgia to Georgia.

No.	Number and Original Location of Graves.		Date of Removal of Bodies.	Final Disposition of Remains.		Remarks.
	Number of Graves.	Original Location.		Number of Bodies.	Final Resting-place.	
294	748	Lawton and vicinity, Ga.,	Nov. 10, 1866, to Feb. 28, 1867.	1,128	Lawton National Cemetery, Ga., on land F. G. Godbee, (Screven county, Ga.)	
295	380	Macon and vicinity, "	Nov. 10, 1866, to Feb. 28, 1867.			
296	26	Griswoldville and Gordon, Ga.,				
297	13	Milledgeville and vicinity, "				
298	78	Macon and vicinity, "	Mar. 9, 1867.			
299	24	" "	Mar. 12, 1867.	187	Andersonville National Cemetery, Ga., on land of B. B. Dykes, (Sumter county, Ga.)	
300	30	Sandersville and vicinity, "	Mar. 25, 1867.			
301	5	Irwinton and vicinity, "	Mar. 29, 1867.			
302	10	Milledgeville and vicinity, "	Mar. 30, 1867.			
303	1	Americus, "	Do. do.			
304	38	Calhoun and Sweetwater, "				
305	28	Adairsville, "				
306	10	Gilmer county, "				
307	8	Social Circle, "				
308	236	Kingston, "	During Oct., Nov., and Dec., 1866.	2,916	Marietta National Cemetery, Ga., on land of Henry G. Cole, (Cobb county, Ga.)	
309	19	Resaca, "				
310	442	Rome, "				
311	343	Kenesaw Mountain, "				
312	655	New Hope and vicinity, "				
313	272	Peachtree Creek, "				
314	587	Atlanta, "				
315	278	Marietta, "				
		Total removed to Cemeteries in Georgia		4,231		

V.—From Louisiana and Mississippi to Louisiana.

316	29	Upper Springfield Landing, La., (8 miles south of Port Hudson; 150 yards east of Young's house)	Dec. 9, 1867.	(Square No. 4.)
317	11	Prophet's Island, (6 miles below Port Hudson, La.; 1 mile S. W. from J. W. Riley's house)	Dec. 11, 1867.	(Square No. 4.)
318	2	East Branch Miss. River, (100 yards N. W. of Dr. J. W. Jones' house, about 4 miles below Port Hudson, La.)	Dec. 12, 1867.	(Square No. 4.)
319	9	Houston Place, (3 miles from Port Hudson, La.)	Dec. 13, 1867.	(Square No. 1.)
320	99	On the Batture, (1¼ mile N. W. from Port Hudson, La., and 50 yards S. of Big Sandy Creek)	Dec. 13 to 16, 1867.	(Square No. 1.)
321	9	Chambers' Place, (6 miles N. W. from Port Hudson, and 200 yards from Mr. Chambers' sugar-house)	Dec. 16, 1867.	(Square No. 1.)
322	12	Houston Place, (3 miles N. W. from Port Hudson, La., and ¼ mile from the Delombré House)	Dec. 17, 1867.	(Square No. 1.)
		Mr. Slaughter's place, (4 of them found 300 yards N. E. from Mr. Slaughter's house, and on the east side of road leading from Mr. Slaughter's residence to Port Hudson and Baton Rouge roads; 3 found 225 yards N. E. from Mr. Slaughter's house on the west side of above-mentioned road, and enclosed by picket fence; 8 found 225 yards N. E. from said house and on the west side of the road already mentioned; 13 found 250 yards N. E. of Mr. Slaughter's house, and on west side of said road; 1 found 250 yards N. W. of Mr. Slaughter's house, ¼ mile on the west side of road above mentioned; 1 found 150 yards S. E. of Mr. Slaughter's house, and 25 yards east of road heretofore mentioned		
323	35	Carried forward	Dec. 19, 1867.	Port Hudson National Cemetery, La., on land of J. H. Gibbons, (East Feliciana county, La.)
				206
				206

From Louisiana and Mississippi to Louisiana—Continued.

No.	Number and Original Location of Graves.		Date of Removal of Bodies.	Final Disposition of Remains.		Remarks.
	Number of Graves.	Original Location.		Number of Bodies.	Final Resting-place.	
		Brought forward... tioned, and 10 yards from two small pin oak trees; 2 found 100 yards N. E. of Mr. Slaughter's house, and on the west side of above-mentioned road; 3 found ¼ mile S. E. of Mr. Slaughter's house, and 25 yards from a small magnolia tree on which was carved the "Union flag; on the right of the flag was "Union forever: Amen," with the name E. Frances, 6th Mich.)		206		
324	8	Ambrose Place, (¼ mile north of Port Hudson, and ⅓ mile from the house now occupied by Mr. Anthony Stuart)	Dec. 20, 1867.	} 86	(Square No. 1.)	
325	49	Taken from inside and outside of the fence around the Cemetery	Dec. 20, 1867.		(Square No. 1.)	
326	29	Woodside Plantation, (3 miles east of Port Hudson, and 50 yards south of Mr. Woodside's gin-house)	Dec. 23, 1867.		(Square No. 4.)	
327	646	Jackson Barracks, La.	Dec. 12, 1866.	} 7,077	Monument Cemetery, Chalmette, near New Orleans, La., (Orleans county, La.)	
328	879	Carrolton Avenue, "	Feb. 20, 1867.			
329	424	Sedgwick Hospital, "	Mar. 14, "			
330	954	Camp Parapet, "	May 4, 1867.			
331	3,449	Cypress Grove, (No. 2,) La.	May 7, "			
332	49	Metairie Ridge, "	May 9, "			
333	448	Algiers, "	July 30, "			
334	228	Ship Island, Miss.	Dec. 4, "			
335	13	Florida St., (near National Cemetery, Baton Rouge, La.)	Mar. 20, "			
336	24	Main street, (opposite Penitentiary,) Baton Rouge, La.	Mar. 22, "			

337	Rear of U. S. Arsenal, (Baton Rouge,) La.	Mar. 23 to April 1, 1867.	840	Baton Rouge National Cemetery, La., on land of Pierre Baron and Miss Simonia Buena, (East Baton Rouge county, La.)
338	Highland Road, (3 miles from National Cemetery, La.)	Ap'l 2 to 3, 1867.		
339	Perkins' Road, (2¼ to 3 miles from National Cemetery, La.)	Ap'l 4 to 13, "		
340	Immediate vicinity of Nat'l Cemetery, La.	April 20 to May 4, 1867.		
341	Shreveport, La.	May 6 to 31, '67.	71	Shreveport, National Cemetery, La., (Caddo county, La.)
342	Marshall, Texas "	May 10 to 20, "		
343	Jefferson, "	May 27, "		
	Removed to Cemeteries in Louisiana.		292 7,077 840 71	Port Hudson. Monument. Baton Rouge. Shreveport.
	Total		8,280	

VI.—From Places in Texas to Texas.

344	Galveston, (earthwork on beach,) Texas.	Mar. and April, 1867.	10	Galveston National Cemetery, Texas, (Galveston county, Texas.)
345	Galveston City Cemetery, " "	April, 1867.		
	Total removed to Cemetery in Texas.		10	

VII.—From Tennessee, Alabama, Georgia, and Virginia, to Tennessee.

No.	Number and Original Location of Graves.		Date of Removal of Bodies.	Final Disposition of Remains.		Remarks.
	Number of Graves.	Original Location.		Number of Bodies.	Final Resting-place.	
346	158	Knoxville, Tenn.,	April and May, 1866.			
347	49	Concord, "	"			
348	12	Sevierville, "	"			
349	6	Strawberry Plains, Tenn.	"			
350	44	New Market, "	May, 1866.			
351	11	Dandridge, "	"			
352	17	Morristown, "	"			
353	15	Bean Station, "	"			
354	13	Russelville, "	June, 1866.			
355	26	Bull's Gap, "	"			
356	18	Blue Springs, "	"			
357	10	Lick Creek, "	"			
358	116	Greenville, "	June & July, '66.			
359	8	Rheatown, "	"	888	Knoxville National Cemetery, Tenn., on land of John Dameron, (Knox county, Tenn.)	
360	1	Fullen's Depot, "	"			
361	7	Limestone, "	"			
362	7	Jonesboro', "	"			
363	3	Johnson's Depot, "	"			
364	5	Carter's Station, "	Aug. and Sept., 1866.			
365	8	Blountsville, "	"			
366	1	Bristol, "	"			
367	37	Rutledge, "	"			
368	3	Clinton, "	"			
369	12	Walker's Ford, "	"			
370	7	Maynardsville, "	"			
371	3	Jacksboro', "	"			
372	3	Clinton, "	"			
373	2	Jacksboro', "	"			
374	52	Knoxville, "	"			
375	8	Kingston, "	"			
376	1	Lewisville, "	"			

No.	Location	Number	Date	Remarks
377	Lenoir's Station, Tenn	1	October, November, and December, 1866.	
378	Henry and Emory College, Va	43		
379	Saltville, "	55		
380	Marion, "	3		
381	Dublin, "	87		
382	Wytheville, "	25		
383	White Springs, "	2		
384	New River, "	2		
385	Abingdon, "	7		
386	Resaca, Ga	1,036	June and July, 1866.	
387	Dalton, "	328		
388	Stevenson, Ala	95		
389	Ringgold, Ga	91		
390	Tunnel Hill, Ga	43		
391	Ringgold, "	42		
392	Chattanooga, Tenn	6		
393	Wauhatchie, "	26		
394	Raccoon Mts., "	6		
395	Kelly's Landing, Tenn	5		
396	Lookout Valley, "	19	August and September, 1866.	2,476 — Chattanooga National Cemetery, Tenn., on land of Joseph Ruohs and others, (Hamilton county, Tenn.)
397	Rossville, Ga	1		
398	Green's Mills, Tenn	1		
399	Chickamauga, "	34		
400	Brown's Ferry, "	1		
401	Tantalon, "	4		
402	Anderson, "	12		
403	Grayville, Ga	14		
404	Chickamauga, Tenn	228		
405	Huntsville, Ala	483		
406	Andersonville, Ga	1	October, November, and December, 1866.	
407	Walker's Ford, Tenn	2		
408	Madisonville, "	4		
409	Columbus, "	1		81 — Cumberland Gap National Cemetery, (since removed to Knoxville, Tenn.,) on land of Mr. — Newly, (Hancock county, Tenn.)
410	Cumberland Gap, "	50		
411	Flat Lick, Ky	24		
	Removed to Cemeteries in Tennessee			888 Knoxville. 2,476 Chattanooga. 81 Cumberland Gap.
	Total			3,446

VIII.—Illinois, Kentucky, and Missouri, to Illinois.

No.	Number and Original Location of Graves.		Date of Removal of Bodies.	Final Disposition of Remains.		Remarks.
	Number of Graves.	Original Location.		Number of Bodies.	Final Resting-place.	
413	1,644	In old ground at Mound City National Cemetery, Illinois.	Not removed.	4,771	Mound City National Cemetery, Ill., (Pulaski county, Ill.)	
414	315	Cairo X roads, upper part of city.	April 8 to April 19, 1867.			
415	200	Birds Point, Mo., opposite Cairo, Ill.	April 12 to Apr. 25, 1867.			
416	671	Paducah, Ky.				
417	1	Cairo X roads, upper part of city.				
418	71	Outside Mississippi levee, at Cairo, Ill.				
419	252	At a point seven miles up the Mississippi river, on the Illinois shore.	April 20 to Apr. 25, 1867.			
420	4	Birds Point, Mo., opposite Cairo, Ill.				
421	23	Fort Holt, Ky., opposite Cairo, Ill.				
422	7	In Kentucky, opposite Mound City, Ill.				
423	107	America, Ill.	April 20 to May 12, 1867.			
424	204	Between Mound City and America, Ill.				
425	626	Paducah, Ky.				
426	500	Columbus, Ky.	May 13 to 23, '67.			
427	74	Belmont, Mo.				
428	7	Between Belmont and New Madrid, Mo.				
429	7	Between Cairo and Mound City, Ill.				
430	12	Fort Holt, Ky., opposite Cairo, Ill.	May 3 to June 29, 1867.			
431	5	In Kentucky, opposite Mound City, Ill.				
432	5	Birds Point, Mo., opposite Cairo, Ill.				
433	12	Cairo, Ill.				
434	20	Commerce, Mo.				
435	4	Metropolis, Ill.				
436	165	Uriah Mann's private yard, about ⅓ of a mile from National Cemetery, Camp Butler, Ill.	October 17 to Dec. 15, 1866.	165	Camp Butler National Cemetery, six miles northeast from Springfield, Ill. (Sangamon county, Ill.)	
437	3,384	City Cemetery, Chicago, Ill.	April 13 to 30, 1867.	3,384	Oakwood Cemetery, Chicago, Ill. (Cook county, Ill.)	
		Total removed to Cemeteries in Illinois.		8,320		

IX.—From places in Missouri to Missouri.

No.		Place	Date	Count
438	24	Patterson, Mo		
439	2	⅜ mile northeast of Patterson, Mo		
440	13	¾ mile east of Patterson, Mo		
441	3	1¼ " west "		
442	5	1¼ " north "		Oct. 3 to Oct. 10, 1867.
443	2	1¾ " northwest "		
444	1	3 miles northeast "		
445	6	6¾ miles north "		
446	1	Bailey's Station, 10 miles north from Patterson, Mo		
447	1	Benj. Chandler's Farm, Butler county, Mo		
448	17	E. Keemis' Farm, near Reeves' Station, "		
449	2	Citizen Cemetery, Reeves' Station, Mo		
450	13	Cemetery at Greenville, Mo		Oct. 31 to Nov. 7, 1867.
451	3	Farm of M. P. Collins, 19 miles south of Pilot Knob, Mo		
452	7	On lot of F. Hileman, between Second and Third streets, Pilot Knob, Mo		
453	1	2 miles northwest of Pilot Knob, (on the Caledonia Road,) Mo		Jan. 20, 1868.
454	1	¾ mile west, on J. W. Hancock's Farm, Mo		
455	1	1 mile west, on land of Pilot Knob, Iron county, Mo		
456	1	2 miles north on Middlebrook Road, Mo		
457	2	Four Mile, Dunklin county, Mo		Nov. 21, 1867
458	2	7 miles north of Four Mile, "		"
459	26	Cemetery at Bloomfield, Stoddard Co., Mo		Nov. 23, 1867
460	10	Daniel Miller's Farm, east of and adjoining Bloomfield, Mo		Nov. 24, 1867
461	9	Round Pond, Cape Girardeau county, Mo		Nov. 27, 1867
462	1	2 miles north of Bloomfield, Mo		Nov. 25, 1867
463	4	Dallas, Bollinger county, Mo		
464	1	¼ mile east of Dallas, Mo		Nov. 14, 1867
465	3	4 miles southeast of Dallas, Mo		
466	3	Jackson, Cape Girardeau county, Mo		Nov. 15, 1867
467	3	Huntsville, Mo		June 20, 1867

Jefferson Barracks National Cemetery, Mo., (Jefferson county, Mo.) 168

Carried forward 168

From places in Missouri to Missouri—Continued.

No.	Number and Original Location of Graves.		Date of Removal of Bodies.	Final Disposition of Remains.		Remarks.
	Number of Graves.	Original Location.		Number of Bodies.	Final Resting-place.	
468	26	Brought forward..................		168		
.....	5	Macon City, Mo...................	July 2, 1867.			
.....	3	In City Cemetery, Warrensburg, Mo.				
.....		In Methodist Church lot, adjoining City Cemetery, Warrensburg, Mo.		36	Jefferson Barracks National Cemetery, Mo., (Jefferson county, Mo.)	
.....	1	5 miles south of Warrensburg, on Clinton Road.	Jan. 22, 1868.			
.....	1	In field (formerly a cemetery) of Mr. L. C. Gould, near De Soto, Mo., adjacent to city limits.				
		Total removed to Missouri.........		204		

X.—From places in Colorado Territory to Colorado Territory.

| ..... | 13 | Camp Wild, C. T.................. | October, 1866... | 13 | Walley's Cemetery, Denver, C. T. | |
| | | Total......................... | | 13 | | |

ALPHABETICAL INDEX

TO

ORIGINAL PLACES OF BURIAL, WHENCE BODIES HAVE BEEN REMOVED.

	PAGE.		PAGE.
Abingdon, Va.	23	Cumberland, Va	14
Adairsville, Ga.	18	Cumberland Gap, Tenn.	23
Alexandria county, Va.	8	Cypress Grove, (No. 2,) La.	20
Algiers, La.	20		
America, Ill.	24	Dallas, Mo	25
Americus, Ga.	18	Dalton, Ga	23
Anderson, Tenn.	23	Dandridge, Tenn.	22
Andersonville, Ga.	23	Deep Bottom, Va	10
Antioch Church, Va.	14	De Soto, Mo.	26
Atlanta, Ga.	18	Dicord Bridge, Va.	14
		District of Columbia.	8
Bachelor's Creek, N. C	17	Dublin, Va.	23
Bailey's Station, Mo.	25	Dutch Gap, Va	10
Bean Station, Tenn.	22		
Beaufort, N. C.	17	East Branch Mississippi River, La.	19
Belmont, Mo.	24	Enoch Church, Va.	14
Bethesda Church, Va.	11		
Bird's Point, Mo.	24	Fair Oaks, Va.	13
Bloomfield, Mo.	25	Fairfax county, Va.	8
Blountsville, Tenn.	22	Fayetteville, N. C.	17
Blue Springs, Tenn.	22	Flat Lick, Ky.	23
Brick-house Point, Va.	14	Fort Fisher, N. C.	17
Brighton, Va	14	Fort Gilman, Va.	10
Bristol, Tenn.	22	Fort Harrison, Va.	10
Brown's Ferry, Tenn.	23	Fort Holt, Ky.	24
Brunswick, N. C.	17	Fort Johnson, Va.	10
Bull Run, Va.	8	Fort Yorktown, Va.	14
Bull's Gap, Tenn.	22	Four Mile, Mo.	25
Butler county, Mo.	25	Fullen's Depot, Tenn.	22
		Fussel's Mill, Va.	9–10
Cairo, Ill.	24		
Calhoun, Ga.	18	Gadsden, Ala.	
Camp Parapet, La.	20	Galveston, Texas.	21
Camp Wild, C. T	26	Gilmer county, Ga.	18
Carrolton, Avenue, La.	20	Goldsboro', N. C.	16–17
Carr's Church, Va.	14	Gordon, Ga.	18
Carter's Station, Tenn.	22	Gordonsville, Va.	8
Chattanooga, Tenn.	23	Grafton Church, Va.	14
Cheesman's Landing, Va.	14	Graysville, Ga.	23
Chestnut Grove Church, Va.	14	Greensboro', N. C.	17
Chicago, Ill	24	Green's Mills, Tenn	23
Chickamauga, Tenn.	23	Greenville, Tenn.	22
Clinton, Tenn.	22	Griswoldville, Ga.	18
Cold Harbor, Va.	12	Hall's Shop, Va.	12
Columbus, Tenn	23	Hanover C. H., Va.	12
Columbus, Ky	24	Harrison's Landing, Va.	9
Commerce, Mo.	24	Henry & Emery's College, Va.	23
Concord, Tenn.	22	Hilton, N. C.	17
Crump's X Roads, Va.	14	Huntsville, Ala.	23
Culpeper county, Va.	8	Huntsville, Mo.	25

	PAGE.		PAGE.
Irwinton, Ga	18	Point Lookout, Md	
		Prince George's County, Md	8
Jacksboro', Tenn	22	Prophet's Island, La	19
Jackson, Mo	25		
Jackson Barracks, La	20	Raccoon Mountains, Tenn	23
Jefferson, Texas	21	Raleigh, N. C	16–17
Johnson's Depot, Tenn	22	Reeves' Station, Mo	25
Jonesboro', Tenn	22	Resaca, Ga	18–23
		Rheatown, Tenn	22
Kelley's Landing, Tenn	23	Ringgold, Ga	23
Kenesaw Mountain, Ga	18	Rome, Ga	18
Kingston, Ga	18	Rossville, Ga	23
King and Queen's C. H., Va	14	Round Pond, Mo	25
King William's Church, Va	14	Russellville, Tenn	22
Knoxville, Tenn	22	Rutledge, Tenn	22
Laurel Hill, Va	10	Salem Church, Va	9
Lawton, Ga	18	Saltville, Va	9–23
Lenoir's Station, Tenn	23	Samaria Church, Va	9
Lewisville, Tenn	22	Sanelersville, Ga	18
Lick Creek, Tenn	22	Savage Station, Va	13
Limestone, Tenn	22	Sedgwick Hospital, La	20
Lookout Valley, Tenn	23	Seviersville, Tenn	22
Loudon county, Va	8	Ship Island, Miss	20
		Ship Point, Va	15
Macon, Ga	18	Shreveport, La	21
Macon City, Mo	26	Smithfield, N. C	17
Madisonville, Tenn	23	Smithville, N. C	17
Malvern Hill, Va	9	Social Circle, Ga	18
Marietta, Ga	18	Stevenson, Ala	23
Marion, Va	23	Strawberry Plain, Tenn	22
Marshall, Texas	21	Summit Station, Va	14
Matairie's Ridge, La	20	Sweetwater, Ga	18
Maynardsville, Tenn	22		
Meadow Station, Va	14	Tantalon, Tenn	23
Mechanicsville, Va	14	Tunnel Hill, Ga	23
Metropolis, Ill	24		
Milledgeville, Ga	18	Upper Grafton Church, Va	15
Montgomery county, Md	8	Upper Springfield Landing, La	19
Morehead City, N. C	17		
Morristown, Tenn	22	Walker's Ford, Tenn	22–23
Mound City, Ill	24	Walley's Cemetery, C. T	
Mount Castle, Va	13	Warrensburg, Mo	25
		Warwick C. H., Va	15
Neuse River, N. C	16	Wauhatchie, Tenn	23
Newbern, N. C	17	West Point, Va	15
New Hope, Ga	18	White House Landing, Va	14
New Madrid, Mo	24	White Springs, Va	23
New Market, Tenn	22	Williamsburg, Va	14
New Point Light-house, Va	14	Williams' Ferry, Va	14
New River, Va	23	Wilmington, N. C	17
North East, Ga	17	Wilson's Landing, Va	9
		Wytheville, Va	23
Olive Branch, Va	15		
Orange Court-house, Va	8	Yorktown, Va	14–15–16
Orange and Alexandria R. R., Va	8	Young's Mills, Va	14
Paducah, Ky	24	Zion's Church, Va	15
Patterson, Mo	25		
Peach Tree Creek, Ga	18	6th Corps Hospital, Va	11
Pilot Knob, Mo	25	18th Corps Hospital, Va	11
Pippin Tree Ferry, Va	16		

ALPHABETICAL INDEX

TO

NATIONAL CEMETERIES WHERE BODIES HAVE BEEN DEPOSITED.

	Page.		Page.
Andersonville, Ga.	18	Lawton, Ga.	18
Annapolis, Md.			
Arlington, Va.	8	Marietta, Ga.	18
		Monument, La.	20
Baton Rouge, La.	21	Mound City, Ill.	24
Camp Butler, Ill.	24	Newbern, N. C.	17
Chalmette, La.	20	New Orleans, La.	20
Chattanooga, Tenn.	23		
Chicago, Ill.	24	Oakwood, (near Chicago,) Ill.	24
Cold Harbor, Va.	11-12		
Culpeper, Va.	8	Point Lookout, Md.	
Cumberland Gap, Tenn.	23	Port Hudson, La.	19
Denver, C. T.	26	Raleigh, N. C.	17
Fort Harrison, Va.	9-10	Seven Pines, Va.	13-14
		Shreveport, La.	21
Galveston, Texas.			
Glendale, Va.	21	Walley's, C. T.	26
	9	Wilmington, N. C.	17
Jefferson Barracks, Mo.	25-26		
		Yorktown, Va.	15-16
Knoxville, Tenn.	22		

Quartermaster General's Office, General Orders No. 21, June 11, 1868.

STATEMENT

OF THE

DISPOSITION OF SOME OF THE BODIES

OF

DECEASED UNION SOLDIERS

AND

PRISONERS OF WAR

WHOSE REMAINS HAVE BEEN REMOVED

TO

NATIONAL CEMETERIES

IN THE SOUTHERN AND WESTERN STATES.

VOLUME II.

> Their own proud land's heroic soil
> Shall be their fittest grave;
> She claims from war his richest spoil,
> The ashes of her brave.

WASHINGTON:
GOVERNMENT PRINTING OFFICE.
1868.

STATEMENT OF FINAL DISPOSITION
OF SOLDIERS' REMAINS, VOL. II.

GENERAL ORDERS } QUARTERMASTER GENERAL'S OFFICE,
No. 21. } WASHINGTON, D. C., *June* 11, 1868.

The following statement of the disposition of some of the bodies of deceased Union Soldiers and Prisoners of War, whose remains have been removed to National Cemeteries in the Southern and Western States, (being the second volume of the same,) prepared in the Cemeterial branch of this office, under the direction of Brevet Brigadier General ALEXANDER J. PERRY, Q. M., U. S. Army, is published by authority of the Secretary of War, for the information of surviving comrades and friends, and for use in connection with the "Rolls of Honor" heretofore published by this Office.

M. C. MEIGS,
Quartermaster General,
Brevet Major General, U. S. Army.

QUARTERMASTER GENERAL'S OFFICE,
WASHINGTON, D. C., *June* 3, 1868.

Brevet Major General D. H. RUCKER,
Acting Quartermaster General,
U. S. Army,

GENERAL:

The enclosed "Statement of the Final Disposition of the Bodies of Deceased Union Soldiers and Prisoners of War, whose remains have been removed to National Cemeteries in the Southern and Western States," being the second volume of the same, and embracing particularly the removals to the National Cemeteries at Antietam, Md., Arlington, Culpeper C. H., Staunton, and Winchester, Va., Andersonville, Ga., New Orleans and Port Hudson, La., and to many of those in Kentucky, Missouri, and Kansas, prepared in this Office under the direction of Brevet Colonel C. W. FOLSOM, A. Q. M., U. S. Vols., is respectfully transmitted to you, with the request that it be printed and distributed for use in connection with the "Rolls of Honor" heretofore issued from this Office.

I am, General, very respectfully,
Your obedient servant,
ALEX. J. PERRY,
Bvt. Brig. General and Q. M., U. S. A.

QUARTERMASTER GENERAL'S OFFICE,
WASHINGTON, D. C., *June* 2, 1868.

Brevet Brig. General A. J. PERRY,
Quartermaster, U. S. Army,
Q. M. General's Office, Washington, D. C.

GENERAL:

I have the honor to transmit herewith for publication, in connection with the "Rolls of Honor" which are published by the Quartermaster General, a second volume of "Statements of Final Disposition of the Bodies of Deceased Union Soldiers and Prisoners of War in the National Cemeteries in the Southern and Western States."

This volume contains, among others, the principal removals to the Cemeteries at Staunton and Winchester, Va., Andersonville, Ga., Vicksburg and Corinth, Miss., Memphis and Stone's River, Tenn., Jefferson City, Mo., and to several of the principal Cemeteries in Kentucky; also additional removals to the Cemeteries at Arlington and Culpeper, Va., and New Orleans and Port Hudson, La.

The removal of 57,141 bodies from 531 different localities to 35 of the National Cemeteries is chronicled in this volume; of which, however, 1,747 bodies were enumerated in Vol. I, but are repeated here for convenience of arrangement, in order to give a consolidated view of all the removals to certain Cemeteries.

The work of removal has been retarded during the last year by freshets in the western rivers, and by the epidemics (cholera and yellow fever) which prevailed in the Gulf States and in the Valley of the Mississippi.

Efficient parties are now, however, in the field, and it is confidently believed that all the important removals will be completed before the first of September next. It is supposed that about 35,000 bodies remain yet to be removed.

Doubtless many graves have not yet been found, although the search for them has been diligent; some, perhaps, will forever remain unnoticed.

But the co-operation of the friends and comrades of those soldiers who died and were buried on remote skirmish fields, or at isolated farm hospitals, is earnestly solicited; and any information of the position of such graves (which may be forwarded to the Quartermaster General free of postage) will be carefully treasured up and promptly acted upon by this Department.

One or two more volumes of this Record may be expected as the removals advance to completion.

I am, very respectfully,
Your obedient servant,

CHARLES W. FOLSOM,
Bvt. Colonel, A. Q. M., U. S. Vols.

TABLE OF CONTENTS.

List of the States from and to which the Bodies of Deceased Union Soldiers and Prisoners of War have been removed.

No.	From places in—	To Cemeteries in—	Number of Bodies.	Page.
I.	Pennsylvania and Maryland	Maryland..	4,695	8
II.	Virginia	Virginia....	2,427	9
III.	Georgia and Florida	Georgia....	851	25
IV.	Florida and Alabama	Alabama....	23	27
V.	Florida	Florida....	99	27
VI.	Alabama, Mississippi, Louisiana, and Tennessee	Mississippi..	10,975	28
VII.	Arkansas and Louisiana	Louisiana..	4,889	32
VIII.	Texas	Texas......	258	37
IX.	Virginia, Alabama, Mississippi, Arkansas, Tennessee, Kentucky, and Missouri	Tennessee..	23,438	37
X.	Kentucky	Kentucky..	2,890	42
XI.	Missouri	Missouri...	6,392	46
XII.	Missouri and Kansas	Kansas.....	204	48
	Alphabetical Index of places from which bodies have been removed	....	....	53
	Alphabetical Index of Cemeteries to which bodies have been removed	....	....	58
	Total		57,141	

I. From places in Pennsylvania and Maryland to Maryland.

No.	NUMBER AND ORIGINAL LOCATION OF GRAVES.		DATE OF REMOVAL OF BODIES.	FINAL DISPOSITION OF REMAINS.	
	Number of Graves.	Original Location.		Number of Bodies.	Final Resting-place.
1	1,919	Antietam battle-field, Md.			
2	3	Berlin, "			
3	1	Bloomington, "			
4	9	Brownsville, "			
5	18	Boonsboro', "			
6	120	Burkettsville, "			
7	1	Cavetown, "			
8	198	Claryville, "			
9	4	Clear Spring, "			
10	196	Cumberland, "			
11	3	Fort Pendleton, "			
12	976	Frederick, "			
13	1	Frostburg, "			
14	11	Fulton county, Pa.			
15	9	Funkstown, Md.	From Oct. 15, 1866, to Aug. 15, 1867.	4,695	Antietam National Cemetery, Sharpsburg, Md.
16	211	Hagerstown, "			
17	11	Hancock, "			
18	13	Keedysville, "			
19	5	Little Orleans, "			
20	4	Locust Spring grave-yard, Md.			
21	3	Maryland Heights, Md.			
22	4	Methodist grave-yard at Sharpsburg, Md.			
23	127	Middletown, "			
24	111	Monocacy Junction, "			
25	6	Oakland, "			
26	7	Oldtown, "			
27	3	Point of Rocks, "			
28	35	Sandy Hook, "			
29	67	Smoketown, "			
30	82	Smoketown grave-yard, "			
31	269	South Mountain, "			

32	1	St. James College,	Md
33	1	Urbanna,	"
34	2	Westernport,	"
35	253	Weverton,	"
36	11	Williamsport,	"

Total removed to Antietam.................. 4,695

II.—From places in Virginia to Virginia.

1	3	McCormick's land, near Auburn, Va.	Aug. 17, 1866.
2	2	Charles Marshal's land, near Barbor's X Roads, Va.	Sept. 8, "
3	2	Bealton, (near)	Sept. —, "
4	3	William Beal's land, near Bealton,	Aug. 31, "
5	2	H. Bennett's land, near Bealton,	June 15, "
6	1	Mr. Downmar's land, near Bealton Station,	Aug. 31, "
7	2	Fox's land, near Bealton Station,	June 14, "
8	2	Mr. Gordon's land, near Bealton Station,	Aug. 27, "
9	2	Mr. James' land, 5 miles west of Bealton Station,	June 6, "
10	2	Mrs. Moorman's land, near Bealton Station,	Aug. 24, "
11	1	Mrs. Moxley's land, near Bealton Station,	Jun. 20 to 26, '66.
12	1	Taylor's land, near Bealton Station,	June 13, 1866.
13	1	Mrs. Whitley's land, Bealton Station,	" 26, "
14	1	Delaney's land, Beverly Ford,	" 6, "
15	1	Dr. Hamilton's land, near Beverly Ford,	" 10, "
16	1	Jane's land, near Beverly Ford,	June 6 to 14, '66.
17	5	Mrs. Jennings' land, near Beverly Ford,	Sept. 11, 1866.
18	1	James Blackwell's land, Blackwell,	" 10, "
19	2	Wigfield's land, near Blackwell,	
20	7	Davis' land, Bristoe Station,	May 21 to 25, '66.
21	17	Dickenson's land, near Bristoe Station,	May 10 to 21, '66.
22	3	Hooe's land, Bristoe Station,	May 25, 1866.
23	5	Dogan's land, near Bull Run,	May 4, "
24	4	Mr. Henry's land, near Bull Run Monument,	Aug. 2, "
25	1	Mr. Starbuck's land, near Bull Run,	Aug. 2, "
26	1	Bustable's land, near Catlett Station,	Aug. 16, "
27	1	Mr. Catts' land, near Catlett Station,	July 4, "
28	1	Miss Dickenson's land, near Catlett Station,	Aug. 15, "
29	5	Mrs. Monck's land, near Catlett Station,	July 3 and 4, '66.
		Carried forward.... 81	81

Arlington National Cemetery, Virginia.
(Near Washington, D. C.)

From Virginia to Virginia—Continued.

No.	Number of Graves.	NUMBER AND ORIGINAL LOCATION OF GRAVES. Original Location.	DATE OF REMOVAL OF BODIES.	FINAL DISPOSITION OF REMAINS. Number of Bodies.	Final Resting-place.
		Brought forward............ Va.		81	
30	2	R. Stone's land, near Catlett Station, "	Aug. 12, 1866.		
31	1	Mr. Waller's land, near Catlett Station, "	Aug. 12, "		
32	1	Mrs. Delaney's land, near Freman's Ford, "	June 23, "		
33	1	Mr. Miller's land, near Freman's Ford, "	Aug. 31, "		
34	3	Mrs. Gaines' land, Gainesville, "	May 30 to Au.1, '66		
35	1	Georgetown, "	Aug. 6, 1866.		
36	2	Mrs. Knox's land, Kelly's Ford, "	June 14, 1866.		
37	1	I. Payne's land, near Kelly's Ford, "	June 15, "		
38	2	Mrs. Kinchlow's land, near Kelly's Ford, "	May 29, "		
39	2	Liberty church-yard, "	June 21, "		
40	1	Mrs. Cinclair's land, Liberty, "	June 19, "		
41	6	Mr. Fennell's land, near Manassas Station, "	May 17, "		
42	3	War's family burial-place, near Manassas Station, "	May 19, "		
43	2	Grove Church, near Martinsburg, "	Aug. 28, "		
44	1	Kinsloe's land, southeast of Marlinsburg, "	Aug. 27, "		
45	1	Mrs. Oliver's land, Morrisville, "	June 15, "		
46	1	Mount Holly Church, "	June 15, "		
47	1	Mrs. Beale's land, near Mount Holly Church, "	June 15, "		
48	1	Brook's land, near Mount Holly Church, "	Aug. 24, "		
49	1	Cotney's land, near Mount Holly Church, "	June 16, "		
50	1	Mrs. Wood's land, near Mount Holly Church, "	June 15, "		
51	2	New Baltimore, "	Aug. 16, "		
52	1	Mr. Conrad's land, near New Market, "	Aug. 2, "		
53	1	Ogiers' land, near New Baltimore, "	Sept. 5, "		
54	1	Mr. Welsh's land, near New Baltimore, "	Aug. 4, "		
55	1	Noaksville, "	Aug. 15, "		
56	2	Orleans, (near) "	Sept. —, "		
57	2	C. B. Shacklett's land, near Piedmont, "	Sept. 8, "		
58	2	Mr. Bennett's land, near Rappahannock Station, "	June 18, "		
59	9	Mr. Bowen's land, Rappahannock Station, "	June 13, "		

11

Arlington National Cemetery, Virginia.
(Near Washington, D. C.)

60	1	Mrs. Bowen's land, Rappahannock Station,	Va.	June 22, 1866.	
61	4	Mrs. Brown's land, Rappahannock Station,	"	June 12, "	
62	6	Burnett's land, near Rappahannock Station,	"	June 13, "	
63	1	Mrs. Moor's land, near Rappahannock Station,	"	June 12 and 13,'66	
64	23	Mrs. Stone's land, near Rappahannock Station,	"	Sept. 5, 1866.	
65	2	Lake Woodward's land, near Rectortown,	"	Sept. 4, "	
66	1	Salem,	"	Aug. 4, "	
67	1	Dr. Stephenson's land, near Salem.	"	Aug. 2, "	
68	1	Mr. Dugar's land, near Sudley Mills,	"	Aug. 4, "	
69	1	Thoroughfare Gap,	"	Aug. 4, "	
70	1	Stover's land, near Thoroughfare Gap,	"	July 23, "	
71	1	Union Mills,	"	M'y 28 to Au. 2,'66	201
72	15	Mr. Detwiler's land, near Union Mills,	"	May 29, 1866.	
73	5	Mrs. Dye's land, near Union Mills,	"	May 28, "	
74	1	Mr. Kinchlow's land, near Union Mills,	"	Feb. 10, 1867.	
75	5	J. B. Markley's land, near Union Mills,	"	May 28, 1866.	
76	1	McClain's land, near Union Mills,	"	July 3 and 4, '66.	
77	2	Warrenton Junction, (near)	"	Jun. 22 to 28, '66.	
78	4	Mrs. Bathright's land, Warrenton,	"	Aug. 16, 1866.	
79	1	Beckham's land, near Warrenton,	"	June 28, "	
80	2	Dr. Fisher's land, near Warrenton,	"	Sept. 10, "	
81	1	A. Fithland's land, 6 miles southeast of Warrenton,	"	June 23, "	
82	2	Mrs. Foster's land, near Warrenton Junction,	"	July 4, "	
83	8	J. J. Hunton's land, near Warrenton Junction,	"	July 2 and 3, '66.	
84	1	Mrs. Morrill's land, near Warrenton Junction,	"	July 4, 1866.	
85	2	Mrs. Parker's land, Warrenton Juneton,	"	June 28, "	
86	1	Mrs. J. Porter's land, Warrenton,	"	June 29,	
87	4	Mr. Rudolph's land, near Warrenton Junction,	"	J'e 28 to J'ly 3,'66	
88	14	Dr. Schumate's land near Warrenton Junction,	"	June 26, 1866.	
89	1	Mrs. Scott's land, near Warrenton,	"	Aug. 16, "	
90	2	R. E. Scott's land, near Warrenton Junction,	"	June 28, "	
91	1	Mrs. Smith's land, near Warrenton,	"	April 29, "	
92	*1	Smith's land, near Warrenton Junction,	"	June 28, "	
93	1	Spencer's land, near Warrenton Junction,	"	June 28, "	
94	1	T. B. Stewart's land, near Warrenton Junction,	"	June 26, "	
95	1	Mrs. Taylor's land, near Warrenton,	"	Jun. 21 to 28,'66.	
96	22	Warrenton Cemetery, Warrenton,	"	Aug. 12, 1866.	
97	1	Mrs. Weaver's land, near Warrenton Junction,	"	July 3, "	
98	2	J. Willson's land, near Warrenton Junction,	"	Sept. 10, "	
99	1	Warrington Springs, Carried forward			282

From Virginia to Virginia—Continued.

No.	Number of Graves.	NUMBER AND ORIGINAL LOCATION OF GRAVES. Original Location.	DATE OF REMOVAL OF BODIES.	FINAL DISPOSITION OF REMAINS.	
				Number of Bodies.	Final Resting-place.
		Brought forward		282	
100	2	Mrs. Bligh's land, Warrenton Springs, Va.	June 20, 1866.		
101	5	Hudson's land, Warrenton Springs, "	June 8, "		
102	1	Isaac Keith's land, near Warrenton Springs, "	Aug. 25, "		
103	13	Mrs. Lee's land, near Warrenton Springs, "	June 7, "		
104	1	Porter's land, near Warrenton Springs, "	June 8, "		Arlington National Cemetery, Virginia. (Near Washington, D. C.)
105	2	Dr. Reed's land, near Warrenton Springs, "	June 22, "	33	
106	1	George Schumate's land, near Warrenton Springs, "	Aug. 25, "		
107	4	Shoemaker's land, near Warrenton Springs, "	June 8 to 22, '66.		
108	2	Mr. Barte's land, near Waterloo, "	Sept. 10, 1866.		
109	1	Mrs. George's land, Weaverville, "	Aug. 11, "		
110	1	Dr. Clark's land, White Plains, "	Sept. 8, "		
		Total removed to Arlington, Va.		315	
1	1	T. Shepherd's, near Barry Ford, Va.	Nov. 27, 1866.		
2	33	James Barbor's farm, near Brandy Station, Va	Oct. 9 to Nov. 19, 1866.		
3	29	J. M. Botts' land, near Brandy Station, "	Sept. 18 to Nov. 22, 1866.		
4	5	Frederick Brown's farm near Brandy Station, "	Nov. 19, 1866.		
5	1	S. Bradford's farm, near Brandy Station, "	Nov. 9, "		
6	4	Coleman Crutch's farm, near Brandy Station, "	Oct. 20, "		
7	4	Wm. J. Fife's farm, near Brandy Station, "	Oct. 17, "		
8	25	John H. Fox's land, near Brandy Station, "	Sept. 17 to Oct. 24, 1866.		
9	1	Mrs. Nancy Green's, Brandy Station, "	Nov. 19, 1866.		
10	8	Mrs. Virginia Green's land, near Brandy Station, "	Sept. 30, "		
11	21	James O. Harris' farm, near Brandy Station, "	Oct. 11 to 25, '66.		
12	1	M. Jonbson's farm, Brandy Station, "	Oct. 8, 1866.		
13	2	John Major's farm, near Brandy Station, "	Oct. 22, "		
14	9	Henry Miller's farm, near Brandy Station, "	Nov. 17 to 19, '56.		

Culpeper National Cemetery, Virginia.
(At Culpeper C. H.)

No.	Name	State	Date	Count
15	Daniel Payne's farm, near Brandy Station,	Va.	Oct. 24, 1866.	1
16	Samuel Proctor's farm, near Brandy Station,	"	Oct. 22, "	4
17	Dr. S. Rixey's farm, near Brandy Station,	"	Nov. 9, "	2
18	John Slaughter's farm, near Brandy Station,	"	Oct. 17 to Dec. 13, 1866.	4
19	George Smith's farm, near Brandy Station,	"	Oct. 22, 1866.	1
20	George T. Stewart's farm, near Brandy Station,	"	Oct. 24, "	4
21	George L. Stewart's farm, near Brandy Station,	"	Sept. 26 to Oct. 8, 1866.	9
22	Mrs Nancy Stone's farm, near Brandy Station,	"	Oct. 8, 1866.	4
23	R. Stringfellow's farm, near Brandy Station,	"	Oct. 23 and 24, 1866.	4
24	Dr. J. P. Thom's farm, near Brandy Station,	"	Oct. 9 to Nov. 20, 1866.	6
25	Charles Wager's farm, near Brandy Station,	"	Nov. 21, 1866.	2
26	Mrs. Jane Wise's land, near Brandy Station,	"	Sept. 19, "	31
27	M. Wood's farm, near Brandy Station,	"	Sept. 20 to 26, 1866.	4
28	A. D. Wood's farm, near Brandy Station,	"	Oct. 22 to 26, 1866.	27
29	John Wood's farm, near Brandy Station,	Va.	Oct. 23, 1866.	6
30	E. W. D. Badager's farm, near Cedar Mountain,	"	Nov. 9, "	2
31	G. W. Bedinger's farm, Cedar Mountain,	"	Nov. 8, "	1
32	Lacy D. Brown's farm, near Cedar Mountain,	"	Nov. 19, "	2
33	Catharine Crittenden's farm, near Cedar Mountain,	"	Nov. 6 to Dec. 13, 1866.	54
34	Charles Crittenden's farm, near Cedar Mountain,	"	Oct. 24 to Nov. 24, 1866.	334
35	Lucy Hudson's farm, near Cedar Mountain,	"	Nov. 20, 1866.	1
36	Robert Hudson's farm, near Cedar Mountain,	"	Nov. 8, "	2
37	Thomas B. Nalle's farm, near Cedar Mountain,	"	Nov. 1 to 19, 1866.	5
38	Patter's, near Cedar Mountain,	"	Nov. 21, 1866.	1
39	J. R. Smoot's farm, near Cedar Mountain,	"	Nov. 8, "	9
40	W. Yeager's farm, near Cedar Mountain,	"	Nov. 8, "	2
41	W. O. Bowman's farm, near Charles City,	"	Nov. 16, "	1
42	Joseph Fray's farm, near Charles City,	"	Nov. 16, "	2
43	N. Lattan's farm, near Charles City,	"	Nov. 16, "	1
44	Culpeper Cemetery, Culpeper,	"	Sept. 22 to Nov. 9, 1866.	59
45	James Baxter's farm, near Culpeper,	"	Nov. 19, 1866.	2

Carried forward 729

729

Virginia to Virginia—Continued.

No.	Number and Original Location of Graves.		Date of Removal of Bodies.	Final Disposition of Remains.	
	Number of Graves.	Original Location.		Number of Bodies.	Final Resting-place.
		Brought forward		729	
46	1	John Beti's farm, near Culpeper, Va.	Nov. 24, 1866.		
47	2	Wm. F. Boyne's farm, near Culpeper, Va.	Oct. 24, "		
48	1	J. E. Biger's farm, near Culpeper, "	Oct. 24, "		
49	4	Edward Digger's farm, near Culpeper, "	Oct. 30 to Nov. 23, 1866.		
50	2	Samuel Feltz's farm, near Culpeper, "	Sept. 23, 1866.		
51	3	W. P. Flint's farm, near Culpeper, "	Oct. 30, "		
52	2	W. Flint's farm, near Culpeper, "	Oct. 17, "		
53	2	Mrs. L. Green's farm, near Culpeper, "	Oct. 30, "		
54	42	W. Grinnan's farm, Culpeper, "	Oct. 30 to Dec. 12, 1866.		
55	14	E. D. Hill's farm, near Culpeper, "	Oct. 17 to Nov. 6, 1866.		
56	3	J. Jameson's farm, Culpeper, "	Oct. 16 to Nov. 10, 1866.		
57	1	Mrs. E. Major's farm, near Culpeper, "	Nov. 10, "		
58	39	Lewis P. Nelson's farm, near Culpeper, "	Oct. 15 to Nov. 19, 1866.		
59	8	S. Rixey's farm, near Culpeper, "	Oct. 26 to Nov. 27, 1866.		
60	2	John Rixey's farm, near Culpeper, "	Nov. 10 to 21, 1866.		
61	1	J. H. Rixey's farm, Culpeper, "	Oct. 17, 1866.		
62	6	Thomas Sherman's farm, near Culpeper, "	Sept. 23, "		
63	1	Henry Shackleford's farm, near Culpeper, Va.	Oct. 23, "		
64	4	John Smith's farm, near Culpeper, "	Oct. 26 to Dec. 10, 1866.		
65	1	Dr. A. Taliferro's farm, near Culpeper, "	Oct. 24, 1866.		
66	1	G. G. Thompson's farm, near Culpeper, "	Oct. 20, "		
67	1	Village Cemetery, Culpeper C. H., "	Oct. 15, "		

No.	Number	Name	State	Date	
68	10	D. Wallach's farm, near Culpeper,	Va.	Oct. 24 to Nov. 14, 1866.	Culpeper National Cemetery, Virginia. (At Culpeper C. H.)
69	4	James P. Yancey's farm, near Culpeper,	"	Oct. 26, 1866.	
70	2	John Yancey's farm, near Culpeper,	"	Oct. 26, "	
71	1	James Yancey's farm, near Culpeper,	"	Sept. 24, "	
72	1	Benjamin Yancey's farm, near Culpeper,	"	Nov. 10, "	
73	2	Gordonsville Cemetery,	"	Nov. 27, "	
74	27	C. W. Beale's farm, near Gordonsville,	"	Nov. 16, "	
75	3	R. B. Hacksau's farm, Gordonsville,	"	Nov. 27, "	
76	2	Dr. J. L. Jones' farm, near Gordonsville	"	Nov. 27, "	305
77	4	Peter Boast's farm, near Kelly's Ford,	"	Nov. 3, "	
78	1	James Boast's farm, near Kelly's Ford,	"	Nov. 3, "	
79	23	J. Kelly's farm, near Kelly's Ford,	"	Nov. 6 to 19, 1866.	
80	1	E. Shackleford's farm, near Kelly's Ford,	"	Nov. 3, 1866.	
81	8	John Stone's farm, near Kelly's Ford,	"	Nov. 3 to 6, 1866.	
82	2	E. Gross' farm, near Liberty Mills,	"	Nov. 27, 1866.	
83	1	Dr. J. Reed's farm, Liberty Mills,	"	Nov. 27, "	
84	1	James Earley's farm, near Madison C. H.,	"	Nov. 16, "	
85	5	Episcopal Church-yard, Madison C. H.	"	Nov. 16, "	
86	1	J. H. Stringfellow's farm, Mitchel Station,	"	Nov. 10, "	
87	1	W. A. Robinson's farm, near Morrisville,	"	Nov. 27, "	
88	3	J. S. Walker's farm, Orange C. H.,	"	Nov. 27, "	
89	4	P. P. Nalle's farm, near Raccoon Ford,	"	Nov. 21, "	
90	3	Joseph Pennell's farm, near Raccoon Ford,	"	Nov. 10, "	
91	1	J. C. Porter's farm, near Raccoon Ford,	"	Nov. 24, "	
92	3	James Garnett's farm, near Rapidan Stat'n,	"	Nov. 21, "	
93	2	T. Nalle's farm, near Rapidan Station,	"	Dec. 11, "	
94	1	S. W. Somerville's farm, near Rapidan Ford,	"	Nov. 24, "	
95	1	D. Payne's farm, near Rappahannock Station,	Va.	Oct. 25, "	
96	3	W. J. Schumate's farm, near Rappahannock Stat'n,	"	Oct. 25, "	
97	1	Thomas Carpenter's farm, near Sperryville,	"	Nov. 27, "	
98	3	John Fletcher's farm, near Sperryville,	"	Dec. 2, "	
99	3	E. W. Kendall's farm, near Sperryville,	"	Dec. 2, "	
100	3	John Miller's farm, near Sperryville,	"	Dec. 2, "	
101	1	L. C. Smoot's farm, near Sperryville,	"	Dec. 2, "	
102	3	Lucy Wood's farm, near Sperryville,	"	Dec. 2, "	
103	8	R. M. Coleman's farm, near Stevensburg,	"	Nov. 20, "	
104	23	E. Hansbrough's farm, near Stevensburg,	"	Oct. 19 to Nov. 14, 1866.	
		Carried forward			1,034

Virginia to Virginia—Continued.

No.	Number of Graves.	NUMBER AND ORIGINAL LOCATION. Original Location.	DATE OF REMOVAL OF BODIES.	FINAL DISPOSITION OF REMAINS.	
				Number of Bodies.	Final Resting-place.
		Brought forward		1,034	
105	6	E. McVeigh's farm, near Stevensburg, Va	Oct. 18 to Nov. 12, 1866.		
106	1	J. T. Norman's farm, Stevensburg, "	Nov. 14, 1866.		
107	18	Mrs. Betty Pease's farm, near Stevensburg, Va	Oct. 18 to Nov. 23, 1866.		
108	23	William Stone's farm, near Stevensburg, "	Oct. 18 to Nov. 14, 1866.		
109	2	O. Stringfellow's farm, near Stevensburg, "	Nov. 20, 1866.		
110	18	J. B. Bibb's farm, near Trevilian Station, "	Dec. 2, "		
111	3	C. Banne's farm, near Trevilian Station, "	Nov. 27, "		
112	1	James R. Dunn's farm, near Trevilian Stat'n, "	Dec. 2, "		
113	12	R. H Gentry's farm, near Trevilian Station, "	Nov. 27 to Dec. 2, 1866.		
114	3	George Grady's farm, near Trevilian Station, "	Dec. 2, 1866.	221	Culpeper National Cemetery, Virginia. (At Culpeper C. H.)
115	12	Elizabeth Hester's farm, near Trevilian Stat'n, "	Dec. 2, "		
116	2	J. G. Hunter's farm, near Trevilian Station, "	Dec. 2, "		
117	1	A. McCall's farm, near Trevilian Station, "	Nov. 27, "		
118	7	Mary Meltor's farm, Trevilian Station, "	Dec. 2, "		
119	10	A. Nutherlin's farm, near Trevilian Station, "	Nov. 27, "		
120	3	G. Ogg's farm, near Trevilian Station, "	Dec. 2, "		
121	1	Wm. P. Perkins' farm, near Trevilian Station, "	Nov. 27, "		
122	3	Wm. Perkins' farm, near Trevilian Station, "	Nov. 27, "		
123	4	J. D. Porter's farm, near Trevilian Station, "	Dec. 2, "		
124	3	A. Terno's farm, near Trevilian Station, "	Dec. 3, "		
125	3	Harriet Thomeson's farm, near Trevilian Sta'n, "	Dec. 2, "		
126	2	H. Thompson's farm, near Trevilian Station, "	Nov. 27, "		
127	36	Charles Trevilian's farm, Trevilian Station, "	Dec. 2, "		
128	7	Cemetery, at Washington C. H., "	Nov. 27 to Dec. 2, 1866.		

17

129	30	John Jett's farm, near Washington C. H., Va.	Nov. 27 to Dec. 2, 1866.	
130	6	G. Miller's farm, near Washington C. H., "	Dec. 2, 1866.	
131	1	L. Stone's farm, near Washington C. H., "	Nov. 27, "	
132	2	W. Brown's farm, near Woodville, "	Nov. 27, "	
133	1	John Crop's farm, near Woodville, "	Nov. 27, "	
134	3	Methodist Church-yard, Woodville, "	Nov. 27, "	
		Total removed to Culpeper		1,255
	2	James Bush's farm, Augusta county, Va.		
	1	Foster's farm, Augusta county, "		
	3	B. Hinckley's farm, Augusta county, "		
	10	Kennard's farm, Augusta county, Va., (400 yards south of house, in pasture lot.)		
	1	Samuel Parm's farm, Augusta county, Va.		
	1	Joseph Peters' farm, Augusta county, "		
	1	J. M. Yates' farm, Augusta county, "		
	1	P. S. Brown's farm, Bridgewater, "		
	2	P. A. Carrall's yard, 9 miles from Bridgewater, Va.		
	1	M. E. Church grave-yard, Christiansburg, "		
	1	Jacob Bower's farm, ¼ mile N. of Connor's Store, "		
	1	Cloyd's Mountain, (west side, 150 yards from pike, on bank of creek,) Va.		
	20	S. Floyd's farm, near Cross Keys, Va., (39¼ rods from house.)		
	90	Kenedy's farm, near Cross Keys, Va., (50 yards from house, under cluster of pine trees.)		
	1	Mrs. Mittenbarger's farm, near Cross Keys, Va.		
	2	Mittenbarger's farm, near Cross Keys, "		
	28	A. Perkey's farm, near Cross Keys, Va., (along north side of Harrisonburg road.)		
	6	Union Church-yard, near Cross Keys, Va.		
	1	W. Cox's farm, 3 miles east of Covington, Va., (½ mile north of pike, near Jackson road.)		
	1	West bank Jackson river, 2¼ miles east of Covington, Va.		
	3	Samuel Gardner's farm, Dry Creek, Va. (500 yards south of pike, and 15 yards from bank of creek.)		
	6	Goodwin's farm, on left bank of Dry Creek, Va.		
	1	Grave-yard at Furrey's Furnace, Page county, Va.		
		Carried forward		184

Staunton National Cemetery, Virginia.
(Augusta county.)

184

3

Virginia to Virginia.—Continued.

No.	Number and Original Location of Graves.		Date of Removal of Bodies.	Final Disposition of Remains.	
	Number of Graves.	Original Location.		Number of Bodies.	Final Resting-place.
		Brought forward.............................		184	
	12	Fayette C. H. Cemetery, Va............................			
	2	Henning's farm, Fayette C. H., Va. (500 yards from pike and same from X roads, under apple tree.)			
	21	P. M. Platt (jr.'s) farm, near Fayette C. H., Va. (600 yards from main road.)			
	55	Cemetery at Franklin, Va. (N. E. corner, near oak tree.)......			
	1	Henry Rexroad's farm, 9 miles from Franklin, Va.............			
	4	R. Goodrich's farm, near Gauley, Va.........................			
	15	Thomas Stockton's farm, Gauley river, Va. (300 yards from pike and 500 yards from bridge.)			
	2	G. W. Effingor's farm, near Harrisonburg, Va. (N. E. corner of farm.)			
	14	Jackson Miller's farm, near Harrisonburg, Va. (In woods, near corner of fences.)			
	2	Ott's farm, ¼ mile from Harrisonburg, Va., in woods. (near Winchester valley pike.)			
	4	Presbyterian church grave-yard, Harrisonburg, Va.............			
	6	Town Cemetery, Harrisonburg, Va.............................			
	3	J. H. Yost's farm, near Harrisonburg, Va....................			
	2	Callahan's farm, Jackson river depot, Va. (¼ mile east of house and 6 yards north of pike.)			
	1	Peter Hinton's farm, 5¼ miles west of Jackson river depot, Va. (150 yards south of house and 20 yards north of Jackson river.)			
	2	Callahan's farm, near Jackson river, Va. (¼ mile east of house, and 60 yards south of pike.)			
	1	Oakland churchyard, near Jackson river depot, Va.............			
	5	J. G. Bell's farm, ¼ mile west of Lewisburg, Va. (200 yards north of pike, and 50 yards east of fence, under oak tree.)			
	5	J. E. Bell's farm, near Lewisburg, Va.......................			
	1	Robert Dickens' farm, 2¼ miles east of Lewisburg, Va........			

19

2	Luray, Page county, Va. (West of grave-yard, near north fence.)		
1	Aman's woods, between Luray and Port Republic, Va.		
3	Grave-yard, east of Luray, Va.		
2	H. B. Hershberger's farm, 2 miles south of Luray, Va. (300 yards west of house.)		
1	J. Schular's farm, near Luray, Va. (North side of private burying ground.)		
1	Allebaugh's farm, near Lacey Springs, Va.		
2	Brook's farm, near Lacey Springs, Va.		
3	J. Good's farm, near Lacey Springs, Va.		
1	Lincoln's farm, near Lacey Springs, Va. (East of pike and ¼ mile from Springs.)		
1	J. Long's farm, ¼ mile east of Lacey Springs, Va.		
3	Pumphrey's farm, near Lacey Springs, Va.		
1	Tate's farm, 4 miles south of Lacey Springs, Va.		
7	T. H. Henning's farm, near Meadow Bluff, Va. (800 yards from pike, and same from X roads.)		
1	T. A. Henning's farm, Meadow Bluff, Va.		
1	William Sharp's farm, near Meadow Bluff road, Va. (300 yards from pike.)		
4	David Tualy's farm, Meadow Bluff battlefield, Va.		
14	D. Tualy's farm, near Meadow Bluff, Va. (700 yards from road, in orchard.)		
1	Williams' farm, Meadow Bluff, Va.		
1	Methodist Church grave-yard, 2 miles south of Mt. Solon, Augusta county, Va.		
3	Mrs. Rebecca Barbour's farm, 3 miles east of Milford, Warren county, Va.		
1	J. Hoffman's farm, 1 mile north of Milford, Va. (60 yards west of Luray and Front Royal pike.)		
1	Monterey, Highland county, Va.		
2	Samuel Carpenter's farm, near Piedmont, West Va.		
60	B. Crawford's farm, Piedmont, West Va. (300 yards from house, and 10 rods from road.)		
17	Myer's woods, Piedmont, W. Va. (300 yards from barn, and 100 yards from house.)		
30	Walker's woods, Piedmont, W. Va. (200 yards from house, and 50 yards from barn.)		
1	L. Garrison's pasture lot, near Port Republic, Va.		
2	Hook's woods, 2 miles northeast of Port Republic, Va.		325
	Carried forward.		509

Staunton National Cemetery, Virginia. (Augusta county.)

Virginia to Virginia.—Continued.

No.	Number of Graves.	NUMBER AND ORIGINAL LOCATION OF GRAVES. Original Location.	DATE OF REMOVAL OF BODIES.	FINAL DISPOSITION OF REMAINS.	
				Number of Bodies.	Final Resting-place.
		Brought forward		509	
	3	Hook's farm, near Port Republic, Va. (In pit, west side of woods.)			
	1	Kimper's farm, between Port Republic and Cross Keys, Va.			
	4	General Lewis' corn-field, near Port Republic, Va.			
	3	General Lewis' meadow, Port Republic, Va. (200 yards northeast of house.)			
	2	General Lewis' wheat-field, Port Republic, Va. (50 rods east of house.)			
	3	John Lewis' farm, 2 miles east of Port Republic, Va. (On the Shenandoah river.)			
	1	Ellen Morris' farm, near Port Republic, Va. (400 yards east of house, in pasture lot.)			
	1	Widow Ongobright's woods, near Port Republic, Va. (4 rods from road leading to Luray C. H.)			
	1	Mrs. Palmer's farm, Port Republic, Va.			
	24	James Patterson's farm, near Port Republic, Va.			
	1	L. Shaver's farm, near Port Republic, Va.			
	1	C. S. Weaver's orchard, near Port Republic, Va. (On Shenandoah river.)			
	4	Kerrin's farm, Rockingham county, Va. (400 yards south of pike.)			
	1	Toll gate, (opposite of) Salem, Va. (20 feet from pike.)			
	1	J. G. Wygal's farm, near Salem, Va. (¼ mile north of Dublin depot.)			
	1	Asylum Hill, Staunton, Va.			
	1	John Brown's farm, Staunton, Va.			
	1	J. R. Stewart's farm, near Staunton, Va.			
	55	Thornrose Cemetery, Staunton, Va.		124	Staunton National Cemetery, Virginia. (Augusta county.)
	1	Henry Miller's farm, near White Sulphur Springs, Va. (100 yards south of Dry creek.)			
	8	White Sulphur Springs, Va. (300 yards from spring, and 12 yards south of Covington and Ohio R. R.)			

21

	5	John Gorst's farm. (120 yards south of house.) } Locality not		
	1	Johnson's farm... } stated.		
		Total removed to Staunton........	633	
1	1	Dr. R. J. Colston's farm, Clark County, Va. (3 yards from south bank of Shenandoah river.).........................		
2	1	McDonald's farm, Cool Spring, Clark county, Va. (125 yards west of Shenandoah river, and 40 yards south of wild cherry tree.).-		
3	1	J. Hardestee's farm, Clark county, Va........................		
4	2	Dr. William McGuire's farm, Clark county, Va. (20 paces west of Shenandoah river, and 35 yards south of Snicker's ferry.).-		
5	1	John Smith's farm, Clark county, Va. (80 yards west of Charles-town pike, and 15 paces from locust tree.)................		
6	1	Wade's Station, W. & P. R. R., Clark county, Va. (8 paces from a culvert, under cherry tree.)............................		
7	1	A. Border's farm, Frederick county, Va. (Under oak tree 180 yards northeast of house, and ½ mile from Saumsville.)......		
8	1	Louis Brent's farm, Frederick county, Va. (64 paces due east of Martinsburg pike.)......................................		
9	2	Benjamin Cooley's farm, Frederick county, Va. (500 yards west of Valley pike, and 1 mile from Cedar creek bridge.).......		
10	3	On same farm. (200 yards east of house, and 30 paces from locust tree.)...		From April 19, 1867, to ——.
11	1	E. Dinkle's farm, Frederick county Va. (On side of drain, 225 yards north of Barryville pike.).........................		
12	1	On same farm. (½ mile northeast of Barryville pike, and 12 paces from two white oak stumps.)..............................		
13	1	Eddy's farm, Frederick county, Va...........................	25	Winchester National Cemetery, Va. (Frederick county.)
14	2	Hackwood's farm, Frederick county, Va. (280 yards southeast of house, and 20 paces from oak tree.).......................		
15	1	Mrs. Heater's farm, Frederick county, Va....................		
16	2	Mrs. A. Kerns' farm, Kernstown, Frederick county, Va. (50 yards east of pike, and 5 yards from apple tree.)................		
17	1	Methodist grave-yard, Winchester, Frederick county, Va......		
18	1	Miller's farm, Frederick county, Va. (1 mile north of Middletown, and 800 yards south of pike.)............................		
19	1	Miller's farm, Frederick county, Va. (1¼ mile southeast of Middletown, under pear tree.)...................................		
		Carried forward..........	25	

Virginia to Virginia—Continued.

No.	Number of Graves.	NUMBER AND ORIGINAL LOCATION OF GRAVES. Original Location.	DATE OF REMOVAL OF BODIES.	FINAL DISPOSITION OF REMAINS. Number of Bodies.	Final Resting-place.
		Brought forward		25	
20	1	James Riding's farm, Frederick county, Va. (104 yards north of locust tree, and 300 yards northwest of Middletown.)			
21	1	John Robert's farm, Frederick county, Va. (¾ mile from Brenstown, under red oak tree.)			
22	2	Samuel Sperry's farm, 1¼ mile from Middletown, Frederick co., Va.			
23	2	Benjamin Stickley's farm, Frederick county, Va. (250 paces south of house, and 17 paces from willow tree.)			
24	1	Tice's grave-yard, Frederick county, Va. (1½ mile northwest of Middletown, Chapel road.)			
25	1	Winchester, Frederick county, Va. (H'd Q'rs 21st U. S. Infantry.)			
26	1	Bolivar, Jefferson county, West Va. (¼ mile south of Potomac river, and 400 yards west of town.)			
27	1	Bolivar commons, Jefferson county, Va. (Near Lutheran grave-yard, beside fence.)			
28	7	Grave-yard, near Bolivar, Jefferson county, Va.			
29	5	Methodist grave-yard, Harper's Ferry, Jefferson county, Va.			
30	1	Public grave-yard, Bolivar, Jefferson county, Va. (8 paces north of William Graham's lot.)			
31	2	H. Hill's farm, Louden county, Va. (60 yards from house, on W. side of Leesburg pike.)			
32	1	L. L. Hill's farm, Louden county, Va.			
33	2	W. Hill's farm, Louden county, Va. (90 yards east of Leesburg pike, under locust tree.)			
34	1	F. Moor's farm, Louden county, Va.			
35	1	N. Silcott's woods, Louden county, Va.			
36	1	Jacob Bushron's farm, Shenandoah county, Va.			
37	2	Mrs. Cline's farm, Shenandoah county, Va.			
38	1	Jacob Emsmiller's woods, Shenandoah county, Va. (20 yards west of J. Rinker's line.)			
39	1	J. Erey's farm, Shenandoah county, Va.			

40	1	Aaron Folley's farm, Shenandoah county, Va. (50 yards from house, near blacksmith's shop.)		
41	2	Jacob Funk's farm, Shenandoah county, Va. (40 yards west of Valley pike, under locust tree.)		
42	16	Michael Graham's farm, Shenandoah county, Va. (150 yards east of Valley pike, and same distance from river.)		
43	2	Michael Graham's farm, Shenandoah county, Va. (40 yards west of river, and 200 yards from Valley pike.)		
44	2	S. B. Hashberger's farm, Shenandoah county, Va. (In a gulley southwest of house, near cedar tree.)		
45	1	David Heff's farm, Shenandoah county, Va. (500 yards west of Valley pike, under walnut tree.)		
46	1	C. Keggey's farm, Shenandoah county, Va. (40 yards northwest of house, and 15 yards from Smith's creek.)		
47	1	Peter Keggey's woods, Shenandoah county, Va.		
48	14	John Koontz's farm, Shenandoah county, Va. (500 yards east of Valley pike, and same distance from river.)		
49	3	I. G. Mems' (jr.) farm, Shenandoah county, Va. (500 yards west of house, and 200 yards east of river.)		
50	2	Mems' bottom, Shenandoah county, Va. (120 yards northwest of saw mill.)		
51	1	Mems' bottom, Shenandoah county, Va. (25 yards east of Valley pike, and 100 yards north of elm tree.)		
52	1	General Mems' farm, Shenandoah county, Va. (400 yards west of Valley pike, on bank of river, near oak tree.)		
53	1	Mems' grave-yard, Shenandoah county, Va.	From April 19, 1867, to ——.	105
54	5	Mount Jackson Cemetery, Shenandoah county, Va.		
55	1	William Myer's farm, Shenandoah county, Va. (Between Oregon Springs and Middleback road, adjoining Seymour's farm.)		
56	6	New Market, Shenandoah county, Va. (Outside of west fence, around old Lutheran grave-yard.)		
57	1	New Lutheran grave-yard, New Market, Shenandoah county, Va.		
58	1	Old Lutheran grave-yard, New Market, Shenandoah county, Va.		
59	1	Rice's farm, Shenandoah county, Va. (1 mile north of New Market, east of Valley pike.)		
60	7	Dr. Rice's farm, Shenandoah county, Va. (75 yards west of Valley pike, and 40 yards south of locust tree.)		
61	1	John Rinker's farm, Shenandoah county, Va. (30 yards east of Ensmiller's line.)		
		Carried forward		130

Winchester National Cemetery, Va. (Frederick county.)

From Virginia to Virginia—Continued.

No.	Number of Graves.	NUMBER AND ORIGINAL LOCATION OF GRAVES. Original Location.	DATE OF REMOVAL OF BODIES.	Number of Bodies.	FINAL DISPOSITION OF REMAINS. Final Resting-place.
		Brought forward		130	
62	1	Levi Rinker's farm, Shenandoah county, Va. (20 yards west of Valley pike.)			
63	5	On same farm. (50 yards northwest of Valley pike, and 400 yards from R. R. depot.)			
64	2	V. Ripley's farm, Shenandoah county, Va. (¼ mile west of Valley pike, adjoining Hawkins' farm.)			
65	1	William Ripley's farm, Shenandoah county, Va. (200 yards west of house, beside pike.)			
66	1	John Rupert's farm, Shenandoah county, Va. (In woods, 40 yards from fence.)			
67	1	William Sibert's farm, Shenandoah county, Va.			
68	1	William Siegle's farm, Shenandoah county, Va.			
69	3	D. Stickley's farm, Shenandoah county, Va. (15 yards west of Valley pike, and 200 yards from Cedar creek bridge.)	From April 19, 1867, to ——.	94	Winchester National Cemetery, Va. (Frederick county.)
70	1	On same farm. (60 yards east of Valley pike, and ¼ mile from Cedar creek bridge.)			
71	73	Dr. I. B. Strayer's farm, Shenandoah, county, Va. (From 80 to 160 yards west of Valley pike.)			
72	1	Moses Tryer's farm, Shenandoah county, Va. (West of house, near corner of woods.)			
73	1	On same farm. (On Oregon road, between Mud pike and Foltz's blacksmith shop.)			
74	1	Mrs. Williams' farm, Shenandoah county, Va.			
75	1	Mrs. Buck's farm, Warren county, Va. (70 yards southwest of R. R. bridge, under an apple tree.)			
76	1	Enos Dinkle's farm, Warren county, Va.			
		Total removed to Winchester		224	

III.—From places in Georgia and Florida to Georgia.

1	2	Abbeville Cemetery, Georgia.	
2	21	Albany grave-yard, "	
3	5	Albany vicinity, Georgia. (On Thomasville road.)	
4	1	Mr. Hill's farm, near Albany, Georgia.	
5	3	Americus Cemetery, Georgia.	
6	64	P. Snber's land, near Andersonville, Georgia.	
7	1	Bainbridge grave-yard, Georgia.	
8	1	H. Robinson's land, Ball's ferry road, Georgia. (In the woods.)	
9	21	Central Railroad, Ga. (Line of Sherman's march to Savannah.)	
10	3	Clinton vicinity, Georgia. (Road to Hill'sboro'.)	
11	7	Near Clinton, Georgia. (On old Macon road.)	
12	28	Columbus Cemetery, Georgia.	
13	3	Covington, Georgia. (Confederate grave-yard.)	
14	1	Judge Harris' farm, near Covington, Georgia.	
15	3	Cuthbert, Ga. (2 in town, 1 west of Court-house, in the woods.)	
16	1	John Josey's land, west of Dublin road, Georgia.	
17	3	Near Eatonton, Georgia. (On Monticello road.)	
18	4	Gordon, Georgia. (Near depot on the Central Railroad.)	
19	22	Griswoldville battle-field, Georgia.	
20	5	Hawkinsville, Georgia. (Citizen's Cemetery.)	
21	2	Near Hillsboro', Georgia. (On Monticello road.)	
22	6	Near Hillsboro', Georgia. (In an old field, on Clinton and Hillsboro' road.)	
23	3	Benjamin Barren's farm, near Hillsboro' Georgia.	
24	1	E. Middlebrook's farm, near Hillsboro' Georgia.	
25	1	Near Irving's X roads, Georgia. (South of Irving's house.)	
26	3	Frank Brown's farm, southeast of Irving's X roads, Georgia.	
27	1	Near Irwinton, Georgia. (Ball's ferry road.)	
28	3	Patrick Ward's farm, near Irwinton, Georgia	
29	2	Louisville road, Georgia. (In field, near a clump of pines.)	
30	244	Macon, Georgia. (Enclosure on Reserve.)	
31	51	Macon, Georgia. (Old Cemetery.)	
32	22	Macon, old Fair Grounds, Georgia	
33	87	Macon, Oak Ridge, Georgia. (Rose Hill Cemetery.)	
34	1	Macon Post Hospital, Georgia.	
35	1	Macon, Georgia. (Southeast of Reserve.)	
36	23	Near Macon, Ga. (Smallpox burial-ground on Atlanta road.)	
		Andersonville National Cemetery, Ga. (On land of B. B. Dykes, Sumpter county.)	648
		From Jan. 1867 to Jan. 1868.	
		Carried forward.	648

Georgia and Florida to Georgia.—Continued.

No.	Number of Graves.	NUMBER AND ORIGINAL LOCATION OF GRAVES. Original Location.	DATE OF REMOVAL OF BODIES.	FINAL DISPOSITION OF REMAINS.	
				Number of Bodies.	Final Resting-place.
		Brought forward		648	
37	1	Macon, Georgia. (Foot of Cherry street.)			
38	1	Near Macon, Georgia. (Liberty Chapel burying-ground.)			
39	56	Near Macon, Georgia. (Regimental burying-ground of 137th U. S. Colored Infantry.)			
40	1	Rice's farm, southeast of rifle pits, Macon, Georgia			
41	2	Mrs. York's land, on Perry road, near Macon, Georgia			
42	7	Madison grave-yard, Georgia			
43	4	Near Madison, Georgia. (South of Eatonton road.)			
44	1	James Russell's farm, near McDonough, Georgia			
45	2	Mrs. Bailey's farm, near McDonough, Georgia			
46	2	Milledgeville, Georgia. (On road to Monticello.)			
47	1	Milledgeville, Georgia. (On road to Eatonton.)			
48	8	Milledgeville vicinity, Ga. (On Thompson bridge road to Sandersville.)			
49	4	Near Milledgeville, Georgia. (At fork of Monticello and Eatenton roads.)	From Jan. 1867 to Jan. 1868.	204	Andersonville National Cemetery, Ga.
50	4	Near Milledgeville, Ga. (On a hill east of Mr. Simmons' house.)			
51	1	Near Milledgeville, Ga. (In a field near Trainor's Mill.)			
52	1	North of Milledgeville depot, Ga. (On a hill, in a thicket of pines.)			
53	1	Mr. Coy's farm, 18 miles east of Milledgeville, on turnpike			
54	3	Fraley's farm, Island creek road, Milledgeville, Ga.			
55	1	Frank Freeman's land, Milledgeville, Ga.			
56	5	Mr. Gibbs' farm, in a trench, northwest of Milledgeville depot			
57	1	Mrs. Mathizer's farm, 18 miles from Milledgeville, Ga.			
58	2	Richard Pickett's farm, on Monticello road, 23 miles from Milledgeville, Georgia			
59	3	Cullen Wood's place, 18 miles east of Milledgeville, Georgia			
60	1	Monticello, Georgia. (Methodist Church-yard.)			
61	8	Frank Hsakell's place, on Hillsboro' road, Sunshine, Georgia			
62	3	Sandersville, Georgia. (In the village.)			

63	2	Mrs. Swint's land, near Sandersville, Georgia.	
64	2	Sandersville, Georgia. (On turnpike to Milledgeville.)	
65	3	Sandersville vicinity, Ga. (Thompson bridge road.)	
66	1	Near Sandersville, Ga. (Near George Power's house.)	
67	11	Mrs. Flournoy's land, near Sandersville, Georgia.	
68	1	Hartlett farm, near Sandersville, Georgia.	
69	2	Stanfordsville, Ga. (Branch of Eatonton and Stanfordsville roads.)	
70	1	Near Tenville Station, Ga. (Towards Irving's X roads.)	
71	4	Thomasville, Georgia. (South of old stockade.)	
72	15	Thomasville, Georgia. (12 in grave-yard, 3 near depot.)	
73	26	Near Thomasville, Ga. (12 miles W. of Bainbridge road, in pine woods.)	
74	4	Thomasville vicinity, Ga. (On Albany road.)	
75	1	Kenyan farm, near Toomsboro', Georgia.	
76	1	U. S. Arsenal grave-yard, Florida.	
77	1	Old Greer place, near Worthville, Georgia.	
78	5	Mr. Hendrick's farm, near Worthville, Georgia.	
		Total removed to Andersonville	852

IV.—From places in Florida and Alabama to Alabama.

1	17	Florida and Alabama, near Pollard, Alabama	Dec. 1867, and January, 1868.	23	Mobile National Cemetery, Alabama. (Mobile county.)
2	6	Post Hospital, and at camp of 15th U. S. Infantry	Nov. and Dec., '67, and Jan. '68.		
		Total removed to Mobile		23	

V.—From places in Florida to Florida.

1	99	Catholic Cemetery at Pensacola, Florida	March, 1868.	99	Barancas National Cemetery, Florida. (Escambia county.)
		Total removed to Barancas		99	

VI.—From places in Alabama, Mississippi, Louisiana, and Tennessee, to Mississippi.

No.	Number of Graves.	NUMBER AND ORIGINAL LOCATION OF GRAVES. Original Location.	DATE OF REMOVAL OF BODIES.	FINAL DISPOSITION OF REMAINS. Number of Bodies.	Final Resting-place.
1	242	City Cemetery, Natchez, Miss.	Jan. and Feb., 1868.	483	Natchez National Cemetery, Miss. (Adams county.)
2	80	City Hospital, Natchez, Miss.	"		
3	126	Vandalia grave-yard, opposite Natchez, Miss.	"		
4	2	Ferry landing, Natchez, Miss.	"		
5	6	Smallpox Hospital, Natchez, Miss.	"		
6	14	Mrs. Murray's plantation, Pine Ridge road, Miss.	"		
7	6	Purnell's plantation, near City Cemetery, Natchez, Miss.	"		
8	4	Fort Rosalie and vicinity, Natchez, Miss.	"		
9	3	State Hospital and vicinity, Natchez, Miss.	"		
		Total removed to Natchez		483	
1	106	Chickasaw Bayou, on Yazoo River, Miss.	September, 1867.		
2	2	Johnson's plantation, near mouth of Chickasaw Bayou, Miss.	"		
3	45	De Soto and vicinity, La. (Opposite Vicksburg.)	January, "		
4	58	Duckport and vicinity, La.	November, 1866.		
5	4	Four-mile Bridge, Miss. (Vicksburg and Jackson R. R.)	January, 1867.		
6	3	Fort Hill and vicinity, rear of Vicksburg, Miss.	"		
7	147	Goodrich's landing, La. (Above Vicksburg.)	"		
8	13	Hall's ferry, rear of Vicksburg, Miss.	March, "		
9	9	Adam Lynde's field, Miss. (Scene of Sherman's assault.)	February, "		
10	1	Anthony's plantation, (opp. of) La. (Bet. Milliken's bend and De Soto.)	January, "		
11	275	Ballard's plantation, La. (Bet. Milliken's Bend and De Soto.)	October, 1866.		
12	51	Judge Barnes' plant'n, La. (Bet. Milliken's Bend and De Soto.)	Oct. '66 and Jan. 1867.		
13	3	Buckham's plantation, La. (Bet. Milliken's Bend and De Soto.)	January, 1867.		
14	82	Gen'l Dennis' plant'n, La. (Bet. Milliken's Bend and De Soto.)	Dec. '66 and Jan. 1867.		
15	7	Hanah's plantation, La. (Bet. Milliken's Bend and De Soto.)	October, 1866.		

29

				Vicksburg National Cemetery, Miss. (Warren county.)
16	11	Lowery's plantation, La. (Bet. Milliken's Bend and De Soto.)	January, 1867.	
17	685	Marshall's plantation, La. (Bet. Milliken's Bend and De Soto.)	Oct. and Nov. '66, and Jan., 1867.	
18	22	McDowell's plantation, La. (Bet. Milliken's Bend and De Soto.)	November, 1866.	
19	29	Meagher's plantation, La. (Bet. Milliken's Bend and De Soto.)	January, 1867.	
20	93	Milliken's Bend, La.	"	
21	325	Morency's plantation, La. (Bet. Milliken's Bend and De Soto.)	"	
22	54	Opposite Morency's, La. (Bet. Milliken's Bend and De Soto.)	"	
23	24	School Section, La. (Near Milliken's Bend.)	"	
24	230	Between Stewart's and Gen'l Dennis', La. (Near Milliken's Bend.)	December, 1866.	
25	13	Col. Town's plantation, La. (Bet. Milliken's Bend and De Soto.)	January, 1867.	
26	9	Young's plantation, La. (Bet. Milliken's Bend and De Soto.)	October, 1866.	
27	51	Col. Young's planta'n, La. (Bet. Milliken's Bend and De Soto.)	December, 1866.	
28	1	Omega landing, La.	January, 1867.	
29	6	Pawpaw Island, La.	November, 1866.	
30	101	Ration Hill and vicinity, Miss.	September, 1867.	
31	12	Baker's plantation, Miss. (Snyder's Bluff)	"	
32	23	Burns' plantation, Miss. (Snyder's Bluff)	"	
33	7	Snyder's plantation, Miss. (Snyder's Bluff.)	"	
34	114	Sprout Spring, (vicinity of) Miss.	March, "	
35	113	Two-mile Bridge, Miss. (Vicksburg and Jackson R. R.)	July, "	
36	1	Vicksburg, Miss.	Nov., 1866, and Feb. 1867.	
37	297	Vicksburg City Cemetery, Miss.	Not removed.	
38	12	Vicksburg National Cemetery, Miss.	September, 1867.	
39	22	Adams' plantation, 4 miles north of Vicksburg, Miss.	Feb. and March, 1867.	
40	44	Baldwin's ferry road, 4 miles east of Vicksburg, Miss.	March, 1867.	
41	2	Brooks' plantation, rear of Vicksburg, Miss.	January, "	
42	94	Dr. H. Cook's plantation, rear of Vicksburg, Miss.	February, "	
43	164	Ferguson's orchard, rear of Vicksburg, Miss.	January, "	
44	34	Grant and Pendleton Monument, rear of Vicksburg, Miss.	Feb. and March, 1867.	
45	39	Hammett's field, rear of Vicksburg, Miss.	March, 1867.	
46	4	Hazzard's plantation, rear of Vicksburg, Miss.	January, "	
47	1	Dr. Jackson's plantation, rear of Vicksburg, Miss.	March, "	
48	49	Magnolia Hall, rear of Vicksburg, Miss.	September, "	
49	20	McGee's land, 1 mile north of Vicksburg, Miss.	February, "	
50	8	Near City Cemetery, Vicksburg, Miss.	March, "	
51	40	Near Four Forts, rear of Vicksburg, Miss.		
		Carried forward		3,560
				3,560

Alabama, Mississippi, Louisiana, and Tennessee to Mississippi—Continued.

No.	Number of Graves.	NUMBER AND ORIGINAL LOCATION OF GRAVES. Original Location.	DATE OF REMOVAL OF BODIES.	Number of Bodies.	FINAL DISPOSITION OF REMAINS. Final Resting-place.
		Brought forward		3,560	
52	16	Near Rebel fort, Vicksburg, Miss	March, 1867.		
53	275	Near Mississippi river, 1 mile above Vicksburg, Miss	October, "		
54	8	Riley's farm, rear of Vicksburg, Miss	March, "		
55	1	Shannon's yard, near City Hospital, Vicksburg, Miss	February, "		
56	1	Dr. Smith's plantation, 8 miles north of Vicksburg, Miss	January, "		
57	99	Sweet's orchard, rear of Vicksburg, Miss	March, "		Vicksburg National Cemetery, Miss.
58	604	Dr. Charles Vick's land near Shirley House, Vicksburg, Miss	Oct. and Nov. 1867.		
59	20	Warrenton road, 2 miles south of Vicksburg, Miss	March, 1867.	1,385	
60	24	Whatley's plantation, 12 miles north of Vicksburg, Miss	September, "		
61	134	Vicinity of White House, rear of Vicksburg, Miss	February, "		
62	66	Willis' plantation, rear of Vicksburg, Miss	" "		
63	137	Young's Point and vicinity, La	December, 1866.		
		Total removed to Vicksburg		4,945	
1	12	Abbeville, Miss	June, 1867.		
2	1	Aberdeen City Cemetery, Miss	July, "		
3	8	Athens and vicinity, Alabama	January, "		
4	1	Baldwin, Miss	July, "		
5	10	Barton Station and vicinity, Alabama	January, "		
6	31	Bethel and vicinity, Tenn	April, "		
7	226	Bolivar Hospital, Tenn	January, "		
8	111	Brice's X roads Miss	July, "		
9	5	Britton's lane, Tenn	" "		
10	3	Bernsville and vicinity, Miss	" "		
11	35	Camp Davies, Miss			
12	2	Canton, Miss	May, "		
13	14	Cherokee Station and vicinity, Alabama	April, "		

				Corinth National Cemetery, Mississippi. (Tishmingo county.)
14	Chewalla, Tenn	32	May, 1867.	
15	Coffeeville, Miss	2	"	
16	Columbus and vicinity, Miss	41	July, "	
17	Corinth and vicinity, Miss	1,554	January, 1867.	
18	Corinth, Miss. (Hospital 150 yards west of College buildings.)	208	"	
19	Corinth, Miss. (Pope's Division hospital.)	291	"	
20	Corinth, Miss. (Hospital at College buildings.)	145	"	
21	Corinth, Miss. (Hospital on widow Hynmar's place.)	15	"	
22	Corinth, Miss. (Hospital on Mr. Irwin's place.)	98	"	
23	Corinth, Miss. (Hospital on Mr. Carter's place.)	9	"	
24	Corinth, Miss. (Buel and Nelson's Hospital.)	121	"	
25	Courtland, Alabama	2	"	
26	Decatur hospital, Alabama	267	April, "	
27	Dixon Station, Alabama	2	July, "	
28	Dunlap Springs, Miss	3	May, "	
29	Dyer's Station, Tenn	1	July, "	
30	Egypt Station, Miss	28	January, "	
31	Elkmont and vicinity, Alabama	62	July, "	
32	Ellistown, Miss	4	"	
33	Farmington and vicinity, Tenn	103	January, "	
34	Glendale, Miss	41	July, "	
35	Grand Junction hospital, Tenn	104	January, "	
36	Hamburg road, Tenn	15	July, "	
37	Harris Station, (vicinity of) Alabama	9	January, "	
38	Hatchie river, Miss	4	April, "	
39	Holly Springs hospital, Miss	118	January, "	
40	Humboldt and vicinity, Tenn	35	"	
41	Iuka hospital, Miss	431	"	
42	Jacinto hospital, Tenn	36	July, "	
43	Jackson hospital, Tenn	538	January, "	
44	Jobe's house, Miss	49	May, "	
45	Jonesboro' and vicinity, Alabama	4	July, "	
46	Kenton and vicinity, Tenn	16	January, "	
47	Kossuth and vicinity, Miss	6	July, "	
48	Leighton and vicinity, Alabama	2	May, "	
49	Lexington, Tenn	7	July, "	
50	Meadow Station, Tenn	3	"	
51	Middlebury Station, Tenn	7	July, "	
52	Miffin, Tenn	1	January, "	
53	Okolona hospital, Miss	106	"	
	Carried forward			4,979

Alabama, Mississippi, Louisiana, and Tennessee to Mississippi.—Continued.

No.	Number of Graves.	NUMBER AND ORIGINAL LOCATION OF GRAVES. Original Location.	DATE OF REMOVAL OF BODIES.	FINAL DISPOSITION OF REMAINS. Number of Bodies.	Final Resting-place.
		Brought forward		4,979	
54	39	Oxford hospital, Miss.	January, 1867.		
55	29	Parker's X roads, Tenn.	July, "		
56	2	Pinson Station, Tenn.	"		
57	20	Pittsburg Landing road, Tenn.	"		
58	32	Pocahontas, Tenn.	"		
59	4	Purdy and vicinity, Tenn.	April, "		
60	30	Rienzi, Miss.	June, "		
61	2	Rutherford's Station, Tenn.	May, "		
62	4	Salem, Miss.	June, "	568	Corinth National Cemetery, Mississippi.
63	1	Saltillo, Miss.	"		
64	80	Sanlsbury hospital, Tenn.	January, "		
65	43	Trenton and vicinity, Tenn.	May, "		
66	1	Troy, Tenn.	April, "		
67	106	Tupello hospital, Miss.	January, "		
68	88	Tuscumbia hospital, Alabama.	"		
69	76	Union City and vicinity, Tenn.	April, "		
70	1	Water Valley, Miss.	May, "		
71	7	West Point and vicinity, Miss.	July, "		
72	3	Road from Harris Station to Athens, Alabama.	January, "		
		Total removed to Corinth.		5,547	

VII.—From places in Arkansas and Louisiana to Louisiana.

1	4	Baton Rouge, La. (¼ mile from National Cemetery.)	March 24, 1868.		
2	48	Near Baton Rouge, La. (On river bank in front of old fortifications in use during the war.)			
3	1	Mr. B. Herbert's lot, ward 2, Baton Rouge, La.	March 27, 1868.		

33

		Place	Date		
4	1	Magnolia Cemetery, adjoining the National Cemetery, Baton Rouge, Louisiana.	April 11, 1868.		Baton Rouge National Cemetery, La. (E. Baton Rouge county, on land of Pierre Baron and Miss Simonia Buena.)
5	116	Camden, Arkansas. (3 miles from town, and ¼ mile from Awachita river.	April 4 to 11, '68.	191	
6	2	Catholic Cemetery, Plaquemine, La.			
7	19	Cemetery adjoining above.			
		Total removed to Baton Rouge		191	
1	2	Catholic burying-ground, near Bayou Boeuf, La.	March 9, 1868.		
2	27	Daniel Morris' plantation, near Bayou Bouef, St. Mary's parish, Louisiana. (Near R. R. crossing,).	March 9, "		
3	2	Mr. Penyan's plantation, near Bayon Bouef, R. R. crossing, St. Mary's parish, La.	March 9, "		
4	210	Bounet Carre, La.	Feb. 26, "		
5	361	Mrs. Brashear's property, Brashear, St. Mary's parish, La.	Feb. 7 to March 9, 1868.		
6	8	Citizen's burial-ground, north of Brashear, St. Mary's parish, La.	Feb. 25, 1868.		
7	1	Mrs. Church's property, near Brashear, St. Mary's parish, La.	Feb. 25, "		
8	172	J. N. Woolford's plantation, near Brashear, La.	Feb. 18, "		
9	7	L. Young's plantation, near Brashear, La.	Feb. 25, "		
10	2	Catholic Church-yard, Chacahoula, Terrebonne parish, La.	March 9, "		
11	200	Donaldsville, La.	Feb. 17, "		
12	::	Franklin Cemetery, at Franklin, St. Mary's parish, La.	March 23, 1868.	1,413	Chalmetto National Cemetery, La. (Near New Orleans.)
13	62	Public burial-ground at Franklin, La.	March 23, "		
14	5	Chambers' plantation, near Franklin, La.	March 23, "		
15	4	Murphy's plantation, near Franklin, La.	March 23, "		
16	6	H. Nurson's plantation, 2¼ miles north of Franklin, La.	March 23, "		
17	2	Troubridge plantation at Franklin, La.	March 23, "		
18	14	Fort Macomb, La.	January 6, "		
19	70	Fort Pike, La.	Feb. 27, "		
20	11	Mr. Himel's plantation, near Labadieville, La.	March 4, 1868.		
21	22	Camp Stevens, Lafourche parish, La.	March 4, "		
22	54	L. L. Johnson's plantation, near Lafourche crossing, Lafourche parish, La.			
23	20	Mrs. Tucker's plantation, near Lafourche crossing, La.	Feb. 23, "		
24	3	T. E. Vick's plantation, 4 miles southeast of Lafourche crossing, La.	Feb. 23, "		
25	114	Mr. Berwick's property, St. Mary's parish, La.	March 4, "		
26	31	Woodruff's plantation, Terrebonne Station, Terrebonne parish, La.	March 3, "		
		Carried forward	March 7, "	1,413	

Arkansas and Louisiana to Louisiana—Continued.

No.	Number of Graves.	NUMBER AND ORIGINAL LOCATION OF GRAVES. Original Location.	DATE OF REMOVAL OF BODIES.	FINAL DISPOSITION OF REMAINS.	
				Number of Bodies.	Final Resting-place.
		Brought forward		1,413	
27	44	Catholic Church-yard, Thibodeaux, La.	March 4, 1868.		
28	69	Episcopal Church-yard, Thibodeaux, La.	March 4, "		
29	2	Lewis Guion's plantation, Thibodeaux, La.	March 4, "		
30	15	Madame De Lanche's plantation, near Thibodeaux, La.	March 4, "		
31	3	Methodist Church-yard, Tigersville Station, La.	March 9, "		
		Total removed to Chalmette		1,546	Chalmette National Cemetery, La.
1	3	Ambrose place, ¾ mile north of Port Hudson, La., and 300 yards west of house now occupied by Mr. Anthony Stewart	Jan'y 20, 1868.		
2	3	Ambrose plantation, 1 mile northeast of Port Hudson, La., and 75 yards north of confederate breast-works	Jan'y 23, "		
3	39	Capt. Cain's plantation, 4 miles south of Port Hudson, La., on west bank of Mississippi river	March 30, "		
4	26	Gen'l A. G. Carter's plantation, 6 miles northeast of Port Hudson, Louisiana	Jan'y 28, "		
5	2	Dr. Dunn's plantation, 22 miles east of Port Hudson, La., and 2 miles northeast of Olive Branch	Jan'y 17, "		
6	10	Mr. Lucas Elam's place, near St. Francisville, La. 16 miles north of Port Hudson, and 1 mile east of Mississippi river	March 27, "		
7	42	Mr. Gibbin's place, 200 yards east of residence, 1 mile south of Port Hudson, and 1 mile west of National Cemetery	Jan'y 17, "		
8	8	Mr. Gibbin's place, 1½ miles southeast of Port Hudson, ½ mile northwest of Cemetery, and 50 yards southwest of road from Port Hudson to Cemetery	Feb'y 7, "		
9	100	Capt. Griffith's plantation, near Port Hudson, La. (In private Cemetery.)	May 29 to 30, '67.		
10	1	Dr. Hayne's plantation, 2 miles northeast of Jackson, La.			
11	1	Hunt place, 3 miles S. E. of Port Hudson, La. (1 mile E. of Cem'y.)	Feb'y 7, 1868.		

		Place of original interment	Date of death	Removed to
12	19	Mr. McVay's plantation, (Holloway place) 3 miles northeast of Port Hudson, La.	Feb. 11 to March 26, 1868.	Port Hudson National Cemetery, La. (On Mississippi river.)
13	6	Mr. J. A. Montagudo's land, 3 miles east of Port Hudson, La. (¼ mile southwest of house.)	Jan'y 16, 1868.	
14	40	Mrs. Montagudo's place, 1¼ mile northeast of Port Hudson, La. (West of house, near confederate breast-works)	Jan. 21 and 22, 1868.	
15	200	Near Madam Montagudo's house, Jackson Sally Port, La	May 11 to 20, '67.	
16	1	James Montagudo's place, 300 yards north of gin house, and 2 miles from Port Hudson, La.	April 7, 1868.	
17	15	Mt. Pleasant plantation, east of Mississippi river, and 3 miles south of Port Hudson, La.	Mar. 20 to 26,'68.	
18	100	Albert Nevil's plantation, 2 miles from Port Hudson, La.	June 1 to 10, '67.	
19	1	Mrs. Newport's plantation, 1 mile east of her house, and 50 yards west of Port Hudson and Clinton R. R., La.	Jan'y 28, 1868.	
20	1	Rondleson place, 1½ miles east of Port Hudson, La. (⅜ mile N. W. of Cemetery.)	Feb'y 7, 1868.	
21	21	Rondleson place, 200 yards east of Mississippi river, south of the Rondleson hotel, La.	Jan. 17 to April 15, 1868.	
22	1	W. S. Slaughter's place, 2 miles east of Port Hudson, and ¾ mile southeast of Mr. S.'s house.	Jan'y 24, 1868.	
23	4	W. S. Slaughter's plantation, 1½ mile southeast of Port Hudson. (In the woods.)	April 14, "	
24	5	Mr. Townsend's place, 6 miles southeast of Port Hudson. (Near Plain's store.)	March 25, "	
25	2	Alex. Wilson's plantation, 6 miles west of Jackson, La. (On road to Bayou Sara.)	April 11, "	
26	6	Woodside plantation, 3 miles east of Port Hudson, La. (Near rebel fortifications.)	Jan'y 16, "	
27	1	John Wrist's place, 1¼ mile northeast of Port Hudson, La.	April 7, "	
28	13	Robert Young's place, 5 miles northeast of Port Hudson, La. (¼ mile southwest of the Plain's store.)	March 27, "	
29	12	On Batture, 1¼ mile northeast of Port Hudson, La. (100 yards west of road to Houston place, and same distance south of Big Sandy creek.)	Jan'y 21, "	
30	6	Bayou Sara, 15 miles north of Port Hudson, La. (100 yards from R. R. depot.)	March 27, "	
		Carried forward		691

Arkansas and Louisiana to Louisiana.—Continued.

No.	Number of Graves.	NUMBER AND ORIGINAL LOCATION OF GRAVES. Original Location.	DATE OF REMOVAL OF BODIES.	Number of Bodies.	FINAL DISPOSITION OF REMAINS. Final Resting-place.
		Brought forward		691	
31	8	Clinton, La.; 6 of them in north corner of burial-ground, 1 north of Clinton and Port Hudson R. R., and 400 yards west of depot, and 1 south of same R. R., and ¾ mile west of depot	April 9, 1868.		
32	15	Fontania, 2 miles south of Port Hudson, and 100 yards west of Springfield and Port Hudson R. R.	January 31 to Feb'y 12, 1868.		
33	1	Fontania, 2 miles south of Port Hudson, east bank of Mississippi river, and 30 yards south of warehouse.	April 15, 1868.		
34	3	Jackson La. (Confederate burial-ground, in the rear of Methodist College.)	April 11, "		Port Hudson National Cemetery, La.
35	100	Near Jackson Sally Port, La. (On Jackson road.)	May 11 to 20, '67.		
36	94	Jackson Sally Port, La. (In the fields and woods towards Big Sandy Creek.)	June 10 to 20, 1867.		
37	5	Jackson Sally Port, La. (300 yards to the northeast and 1½ mile from Port Hudson.)	Jan'y 23, 1868.	2,347	
38	696	Morganza, La., 30 miles above Port Hudson, on the west bank of Mississippi river.	February 17 to 29, 1868.		
39	146	Mt. Pleasant Landing, La. (2 miles south of the present National Cemetery.)	May 1 to 10, '67.		
40	1,211	Port Hudson, La. (Within the limits, and in the immediate vicinity of the present National Cemetery.)	April 3, 1867, to Jan'y 18, '68.		
41	10	Port Hudson, La. (¼ mile northeast of town, and 200 yards northwest of confederate salt works.)	July 24, 1868.		
42	58	Port Hudson, La. (Fields and woods around confederate breastworks.)	Mar. 10 to 18, '63.		
		Total removed to Port Hudson		3,038	

37

1	Cheneyville, La	3		April 4, 1868.	
2	Clear creek, "	6		April 4, "	
3	Compton's plantation, La	1		March 8, "	
4	Fort DeRussey, "	18		March 8, "	Alexandria National Cemetery, La. (Rapides county, on Red river.)
5	Irou's plantation, "	2		April 4, "	
6	Dr. Slaughter's plantation, La.	1		March 8, "	
7	Smith's plantation, "	6		March 8, "	
8	Wilson's landing, "	1		March 8, "	
9	Yellow Bayou and vicinity, "	76		March 6, "	
	Total removed to Alexandria		114		

VIII.—From places in Texas to Texas.

1	Military Cemeteries at Indianola, Texas, and Victoria and vicinity	258		Mar. 23–30, 1868.	Brownsville National Cemetery, Texas. (Near mouth of Rio Grande.)
	Total removed to Brownsville		258		

IX.—From places in Virginia, Alabama, Mississippi, Arkansas, Tennessee, Kentucky, and Missouri, to Tennessee.

1	Abingdon, Va	10			
2	Adkin's Switch, Va	4			
3	Barboursville road, Ky	3			
4	Bean Station, Tenn	15			
5	Big Creek Gap, "	3			Knoxville National Cemetery, Tenn. (Knox county, on land of John Dameron.)
6	Blountville, "	8		From May 7, 1867, to March 16, 1868.	
7	Blue Springs, "	17			
8	Bristol, "	1			
9	Bulls Gap, "	27			
10	Bulls Gap road, Va	3			
11	Campbell's Station road, Tenn	2			
12	Carter's Station, Tenn	5			
	Carried forward		98		

Virginia, Alabama, Mississippi, Arkansas, Tennessee, Kentucky, and Missouri, to Tennessee.—Continued.

No.	NUMBER AND ORIGINAL LOCATION OF GRAVES.		DATE OF REMOVAL OF BODIES.	FINAL DISPOSITION OF REMAINS.	
	Number of Graves.	Original Location.		Number of Bodies.	Final Resting-place.
		Brought forward		98	
13	3	Clear Creek, Tenn			
14	7	Clinton, "			
15	1	Columbus, "			
16	53	Concord, "			
17	278	Cumberland Gap, Tenn			
18	63	Cumberland Ford, Ky			
19	27	Cumberland River, Ky			
20	19	Dandridge, Tenn			
21	90	Dublin, Va			
22	85	Flat Lick, Ky			
23	2	Goose Creek road, Tenn			
24	74	Greenville, Tenn	From May 7, 1867, to March 16, 1868.	3,049	Knoxville National Cemetery, Tenn., (Knox co., on land of John Dameron.)
25	49	Henry and Emory College, Va			
26	20	Jacksboro', Tenn			
27	5	Jacksboro' road, Tenn			
28	4	Johnson's depot, "			
29	8	Jonesboro', "			
30	15	Joneville, Va			
31	8	Kingston, Tenn			
32	1,853	Knoxville, Tenn			
33	1	Lenoir's Station, Tenn			
34	10	Lick Creek, "			
35	6	Limestone, "			
36	6	Louden, "			
37	1	Louisville, "			
38	4	Madisonville, "			
39	13	Marion, Va			
40	7	Maynardsville, Tenn			
41	17	Morristown, "			
42	30	Mosey creek, "			

43	Mount Airy, Va	2	
44	New Market, Tenn	18	
45	New River bridge, Va	2	
46	Poor Valley ridge, Ky	28	
47	Rheatown, Tenn	10	
48	Russelville, Tenn	13	
49	Rutledge, Tenn	32	
50	Saltville, Va	66	
51	Sevierville, Tenn	14	
52	Sinking Creek, Ky	1	
53	Strawberry Plains, Tenn	8	
54	Tazewell and vicinity, Tenn	59	
55	Walker's Ford, Tenn	12	
56	White Springs, Va	2	
57	Wytheville, Va	30	
	Total removed to Knoxville		3,147
1	Brownsville, Tenn	1	
2	Brownsville and Fulton road, Tenn	1	
3	Brownsville and Jackson road, Tenn	1	
4	Black Fish lake, Miss	62	
5	Coldwater river, (mouth of) Miss	4	
6	Clandestine House, near Helena, Ark	45	
7	Collierville and vicinity, Tenn	84	
8	Elmwood Cemetery, Tenn	759	
9	Fort Hindman, (near) Ark	320	
10	Fort Pillow, Tenn	243	
11	Fort Pickering, Tenn	250	Memphis National Cemetery, Tenn. (On Mississippi river.) From April, 1867, to February, 1868. 3,133
12	Fisherville, (east of) Tenn	2	
13	Fort Curtis, near Helena, Ark	215	
14	Humboldt road, Tenn	1	
15	Hackman, Tenn	13	
16	Helena and vicinity, Ark	930	
17	Hawk House, near Helena, Ark	85	
18	Island No. 10	18	
19	Island No. 40	3	
20	Isler Landing, Tenn	27	
21	Lacopolis, Miss	19	
	(Carried forward)		3,153

Virginia, Alabama, Mississippi, Arkansas, Tennessee, Kentucky, and Missouri, to Tennessee—Continued.

No.	Number of Graves.	NUMBER AND ORIGINAL LOCATION OF GRAVES. Original Location.	DATE OF REMOVAL OF BODIES.	FINAL DISPOSITION OF REMAINS. Number of Bodies.	Final Resting-place.
		Brought forward		3,133	
22	460	Little Rock road, Ark			
23	7	La Fayette, Tenn			
24	605	La Grange and vicinity, Tenn			
25	7,097	Memphis Cemetery, (Soldiers') Tenn			
26	1,201	Memphis and vicinity, Tenn			
27	3	Mount Vernon, Tenn			
28	1	Moscow, (vicinity of) Tenn			
29	14	Mason Station, (south of) Tenn			
30	20	Near M. and O. R. R., Tenn			
31	1	Mount Pleasant, Tenn	From April, 1867, to February, 1868.	10,427	Memphis National Cemetery, Tenn. (On Mississippi river.)
32	148	New Madrid, Mo			
33	13	Osceola, Mo			
34	7	Point Pleasant, Mo			
35	42	Paris, (vicinity of) Tenn			
36	560	Saint Frances' road, Ark			
37	128	Saint Frances' road, (south of) Ark			
38	80	Thompson House, near Helena, Ark			
39	7	Tiptonville, Tenn			
40	1	Union depot, (south of) Tenn			
41	5	Wolf river, Tenn			
42	6	Wolf River bridge, Tenn			
43	20	Wyatt and vicinity, Miss			
44	1	West of Union depot, Tenn			
		Total removed to Memphis		13,560	
1	2	Alexandria, Tenn			
2	15	Ashton Mill, Tenn			
3	106	Athens and vicinity, Ala			

4	Athens Cemetery, Ala	73		
5	Bell Buckle, Tenn	3		
6	Bradyville, Tenn	2		
7	Branchville, Tenn	1		
8	Carter's place, Tenn	321		
9	Cipple creek, Tenn	4		
10	Columbia and vicinity, Tenn	294		
11	Columbia pike, Tenn	22		
12	Columbia Male College, Tenn	26		
13	Columbia, (north of) Tenn	33		
14	Cowan, Tenn	48		
15	Cowan grave-yard, Tenn	2		
16	Cowan's plantation, Tenn	51		
17	Decherd, Tenn	35		
18	Elk river, Tenn	2		
19	Estell Springs, Tenn	12		
20	Farmington, Tenn	4	During 1866 and 1867.	4,270	Stone's River National Cemetery, Tenn. (Rutherford county.)
21	Fayetteville, Tenn	17		
22	Fort Rosecrans, Tenn	6		
23	Franklin and vicinity, Tenn	435		
24	Franklin Cemetery, Tenn	231		
25	Franklin battlefield, Tenn	138		
26	Gun spring, Tenn	1		
27	Harding house, Tenn	3		
28	Hickory hill, Tenn	1		
29	Hillsboro' Cemetery, Tenn	7		
30	Hoover's gap, Tenn	18		
31	Lavergne, Tenn	30		
32	Lebanon, Tenn	12		
33	Liberty gap, Tenn	15		
34	Manchester, Tenn	11		
35	Manny's grove, Tenn	1		
36	McGraw's farm, Tenn	26		
37	McKey's residence, (near) Tenn	78		
38	McMinnville, Tenn	2,138		
39	Murfreesboro' and vicinity, Tenn	4		
40	Murfreesboro' grave-yard, Tenn	32		
41	N. and D. R. R., (beside) Tenn	7		
42	Nashville pike, Tenn	2		
43	Normandy, Tenn			
	Carried forward			4,270

Virginia, Alabama, Mississippi, Arkansas, Tennessee, Kentucky, and Missouri, to Tennessee—Continued.

No.	Number of Graves.	NUMBER AND ORIGINAL LOCATION OF GRAVES. Original Location.	DATE OF REMOVAL OF BODIES.	FINAL DISPOSITION OF REMAINS. Number of Bodies.	Final Resting-place.
		Brought forward		4,270	
44	8	Overton's family grave-yard, Tenn.			
45	7	Pulaski, Tenn.			
46	90	Pulaski Cemetery, Tenn.			
47	9	Pulaski pike, Tenn.			
48	27	Readyville, Tenn.			
49	2	Scull Camp bridge, Tenn.			
50	46	Shelbyville, Tenn.			
51	4	Silver Spring, Tenn.	During 1866 and 1867.	2,461	Stone's River National Cemetery, Tenn. (Rutherford county.)
52	4	Sparta, Tenn.			
53	27	Spring hill, (east of) Tenn.			
54	1,835	Stone's river battlefield, Tenn.			
55	3	Stone's river, (near) Tenn.			
56	21	Stone's River National Cemetery, Tenn.			
57	75	Thompson's Station, Tenn.			
58	279	Tullahoma, Tenn.			
59	17	Wartrace, Tenn.			
60	5	Winchester, Tenn.			
61	2	Woodbury, Tenn.			
		Total removed to Stone's River		6,731	
1	1,466	Camp Nelson, Ky.			
2	66	Small-pox Hospital, bank of Kentucky river, west of Camp Nelson, Ky.			
3	1	Little Hickman river, 3 miles east of Camp Nelson, Ky.	During Feb'y, March, April, and May, 1867.	1,654	Camp Nelson National Cemetery, Ky.
4	27	Lancaster Cemetery, Ky.			
5	1	Methodist Chapel, Lexington and Danville pike, Ky.			
6	34	Nicholasville Cemetery, Ky.			
7	2	Sugar Creek road, 5 miles from Nicholasville, Ky.			

43

No.		Count	Location	Total	Notes
8	Stanford Cemetery, Ky.	54			
9	Knoblock turnpike, 2 miles from Stanford, Ky.	1			
10	Somerset road, 5 miles from Stanford, Ky.	2			
	Total removed to Camp Nelson			1,654	
1	Bardstown, Ky. (Near old Woolen Factory)	5			
2	Bardstown Protestant Cemetery, Ky.	236			
3	Bardstown Catholic Cemetery, Ky.	1			
4	Springfield pike, 7 miles from Bardstown, Ky.	1			
5	Wm. Richie's place, 5 miles from Bardstown, Ky.	1			
6	N. Willington's place, Bardstown, Ky.	2			
7	B. Coomb's place, Bardstown, Ky.	10			
8	J. B. Bowman's place, Bardstown, Ky.	45			
9	Bethel Church-yard, Ky.	3			
10	Citizens' Grave-yard, Campbellville, Ky.	28			
11	Old Hazard farm, Campbellville, Ky.	2			
12	Camp Wickliffe, Ky.	2			
13	Cane Valley, (Campbellville and Columbia pike,) Ky.	1			
14	Jos. Kniffley's farm, Casey's creek, Ky.	2			
15	Crab Orchard, Ky. (Town Cemetery)	52			
16	Alex. Frost's place, 6 miles from Crab Orchard, Ky.	1			
17	M. J. Harris' place, Crab Orchard, Ky.	16			
18	James Howard's farm, Crab Orchard, Ky.	1	From April, 1867, to October, 1867.	841	Lebanon National Cemetery, Ky. (Nelson county.)
19	Fredericktown, Ky. (On Bardstown and Springfield pike)	1			
20	Green River bridge, Ky. (On Campbellville and Columbia pike)	10			
21	James Lubbitt's place, Green River bridge, Ky.	1			
22	Greensburg, Ky. (Old Town Cemetery)	389			
23	Lebanon Hospital burials, Ky. (Not removed)	16			
24	Lebanon Town Cemetery, Ky.	1			
25	Bradfordsville road, 7 miles from Lebanon, Ky.	1			
26	Big South Rolling Fork, 18 miles from Lebanon, Ky.	1			
27	Danville road, 2 miles from Lebanon, Ky.	1			
28	W. Abell's farm, 6 miles from Lebanon, Ky.	1			
29	J. E. Fundy's place, Lebanon and Campbellville pike, Ky.	1			
30	Felix Mercer's place, Lebanon, Ky.	3			
31	Liberty, (scattered) Ky.	1			
32	J. Sweeny's burial-ground, Liberty, Ky.	4			
33	Tabernacle Grave-yard, Neatsville, Ky.				
	Carried forward			841	

Virginia, Alabama, Mississippi, Arkansas, Tennessee, Kentucky, and Missouri, to Tennessee—Continued.

No.	Number of Graves.	NUMBER AND ORIGINAL LOCATION OF GRAVES. Original Location.	DATE OF REMOVAL OF BODIES.	FINAL DISPOSITION OF REMAINS.	
				Number of Bodies.	Final Resting-place.
34	2	Billy Williams' Grave-yard, Nealsville, Ky.	From April, 1867, to October, 1867.	841	Lebanon National Cemetery, Ky. (Nelson county.)
35	6	Pleasant Grove Church, New Haven, Ky.			
36	4	J. McDouglas' place, New Haven, Ky.		24	
37	4	G. Smith and J. Friend's farms, New Haven, Ky.			
38	8	New Market, Ky. (Old Baptist Church-yard.)			
		Total removed to Lebanon		865	
1	3	On London road, near Barbourville, Ky.	No date	269	London National Cemetery, Ky. (Laurel county.)
2	3	Methodist Church-yard, vicinity of Barbourville, Ky.			
3	60	Mr. Anderson's farm, Barbourville, Ky.			
4	6	Mr. Black's family grave-yard, near Barbourville, Ky.			
5	1	Brogin's family grave-yard, near Barbourville, Ky.			
6	2	J. P. Ford's grave-yard, old Barbourville road, Ky.			
7	1	A. J. Kane's farm, near Barbourville, Ky.			
8	10	Mr. Sawyer's grave-yard, Barbourville, Ky.			
9	6	Big Hill, Ky. (London and Richmond road.)			
10	1	Boston Town Cemetery, Ky.			
11	2	G. W. Faulkner's family grave-yard, near Boston, Ky.			
12	2	Thos. Perkin's family grave-yard, near Boston, Ky.			
13	1	Near Camp Pitman, Ky. (On Crab Orchard road)			
14	14	Near Camp Pitman, Ky. (On Richmond road)			
15	1	Grave-yard on London and Williamsburg road, Ky.			
16	2	Meeting-house, 14 miles from London, Ky.			
17	3	State Hill Church-yard, vicinity of London, Ky.			
18	1	J. Brangkton's place, 10 miles from London, Ky.			
19	1	Moses Camper's place, 11 miles from London, Ky.			
20	1	Mrs. Carrier's farm, near London, Ky.			
21	2	James Cooper's farm, London and Somerset road, Ky.			

45

22	1	James Dee's farm, near London, Ky.
23	1	At Tom Fairbrush's house, 13 miles from London, Ky.
24	3	R. P. Gresham's family grave-yard, 15 miles from London, Ky.
25	1	Mr. Griffith's farm, 14 miles south of London, Ky.
26	73	General J. Jackson's farm, London, Ky.
27	1	Mr. McHurgue's farm, 16 miles from London, Ky. (Barboursville road)
28	5	John Perkin's place, 14 miles from London, Ky.
29	4	C. P. Wilson's farm, 11 miles from London, Ky.
30	1	Mrs. Lettie Rice's family grave-yard, Manchester, Ky.
31	18	Mount Vernon Cemetery, Ky.
32	7	Crab Orchard road, vicinity of Mount Vernon, Ky.
33	4	Dr. Jopling's and Mr. Ward's, near Mount Vernon, Ky.
34	3	Mr. Owen's place, near Mount Vernon, Ky.
35	1	Judge Pearl's place, near Mount Vernon, Ky.
36	2	White Cat, Ky. (13 miles from London).
37	19	Williamsburg, Ky. (Town Cemetery).
38	2	Wolf Creek grave-yard, vicinity of Williamsburg, Ky.
	269	Total removed to London
1	1	Dan'l Baker's farm, Bakerton road, Ky.
2	1	Widow Carter's farm, Bakerton road, Ky.
3	5	Burkesville, Ky.
4	4	M. Alexander's farm, 7 miles west of Burkesville, Ky.
5	1	Mrs. M. Curtis' farm, 2 miles northeast of Burkesville, Ky.
6	1	Benj. Vaughn's farm, 2 miles northeast of Burkesville, Ky.
7	1	Centre Point, Ky.
8	1	Centreville, Ky.
9	3	Columbia, Ky.
10	2	Bowling Green, 1 mile west of Glasgow, Ky.
11	65	Scottsville Pike, 1 mile southeast of Glasgow, Ky.
12	1	A. Dipp's farm, ¼ mile southeast of Glasgow, Ky.
13	1	Mrs. Kase's farm, 1 mile east of Glasgow, Ky.
14	1	Wm. Neal's farm, 5 miles northeast of Glasgow, Ky.
15	4	Redding's farm, 2 miles south of Glasgow, Ky.
16	1	Pleasant Hill, 12 miles west of Burkesville, Ky.
17	12	Tompkinsville and vicinity, Ky.
18	1	Glasgow road, 3 miles northwest of Tompkinsville, Ky.
	106	Carried forward	During July and August, 1867. Tompkinsville National Cemetery, Ky. (Monroe county.) 106

Virginia, Alabama, Mississippi, Arkansas, Tennessee, Kentucky, and Missouri, to Tennessee—Continued.

No.	Number of Graves.	NUMBER AND ORIGINAL LOCATION OF GRAVES. Original Location.	DATE OF REMOVAL OF BODIES.	FINAL DISPOSITION OF REMAINS. Number of Bodies.	Final Resting-place.
		Brought forward		106	
19	1	Mount Zion Church, 2 miles northeast of Tompkinsville, Ky	During July and August, 1867.	6	Tompkinsville National Cemetery, Ky. (Monroe county.)
20	2	Charles Brown's farm, 12 miles west of Tompkinsville, Ky			
21	2	J. A. Register's farm, 9 miles west of Tompkinsville, Ky			
22	1	Sam'l Thomas' farm, 1 mile southwest of Tompkinsville, Ky			
		Total removed to Tompkinsville		112	
1	14	Cemetery ¼ mile south of Franklin, Franklin county, Mo	March 7, 1868.		
2	2	200 feet north of public school-house, Franklin, Mo	March 7, "		
3	1	Mr. Calvin's lot, 1 mile west of R. R. depot, Franklin, Mo	March 7, "		
4	11	Methodist Church Cemetery, near Hannibal, Mo	March 19, "		
5	26	Cemetery at Houston, Texas county, Mo	March 22, "		
6	1	Field ¼ mile west of Houston, Mo	March 22, "		
7	3	Woods ¼ mile east of Houston, Mo	March 22, "		
8	138	G. Canne's farm, 6 miles west of Houston, Mo	March 23, "		
9	2	Ironton Cemetery, at Ironton, Mo	Jan'y 16, "		
10	1	Near Ironton, Mo. (E. side of Shepard Mount'n, on Pilot Knob road)	Jan'y 16, "		
11	1	¼ mile northeast of Ironton, Mo	Jan'y 16, "		
12	1	400 yards east of Ironton Hotel, Ironton, Mo	Jan'y 16, "		
13	1	¼ mile southeast of Ironton, Mo	Jan'y 16, "		
14	2	Masons' and Odd Fellows' Cemetery, Ironton, Mo	Jan'y 16, "		
15	1	Giles Russell's farm, 300 yards east of Ironton, Mo	Jan'y 16, "		
16	21	Mrs. Wm. Russett's farm, ¼ mile east of Ironton, Mo	Jan'y 16, "		
17	1	Mrs. Shepard's lot, east of and adjoining Ironton, Mo	Jan'y 16, "		
18	22	Near Lake Springs, Mo. (Dent county)	March 14, "		
19	1	J. W. Reed's farm, 8 miles north of Licking, Mo	March 24, "		
20	1	Wm. West's farm, 3 miles north of Licking, Texas county, Mo	March 24, "		
21	1	Moselle Station, Mo. (1 mile east and 20 feet south of southwest Pacific R. R. track)	March 7, "		

22	323	Cemetery at Rolla, Phelps county, Mo.	March 7,		Jefferson Barracks Nat'l Cemetery, Mo. (Jefferson county.)
23	5	3 miles southwest of Rolla, Mo. (Near new Springfield road)	March 12, "		
24	3	10 miles southwest of Rolla, Mo. (Near Hartsville road)	March 24, "		
25	39	H. A. Gagger's farm, 2¼ miles west of Rolla, Mo.	March 9, "		
26	13	H. A. Gody's farm, 2¼ miles west of Rolla, Mo.	March 10, "		
27	4	J. H. Mitchell's farm, 3 miles southeast of Rolla, Mo.	March 12, "		
28	1	Ruggles' farm, 3¼ miles southwest of Rolla, Mo.	March 10, "		
29	15	Cemetery at Salem, Dent county, Mo.	March 18, "		
30	376	Christ Church Cemetery, Saint Louis, Mo.	Feb'y 29, "		
31	3,717	Wesleyan Cemetery, Saint Louis, Mo.	Feb'y 6, "		
32	2	Fulbright Springs, Springfield, Mo.	March 25, "		
33	110	Grave-yard ¼ mile northeast of Court-house at Springfield, Mo.	March 20, "		
34	3	Post Cemetery, near Springfield, Mo.	March 25, "		
35	2	J. McCraw's private burying-ground, 10 miles E. of Springfield, Mo.	March 25, "		
36	6	3 miles north of Syracuse, Mo. (Near Glasgow School-house, Cooper county).	March 10, "		
37	64	Cemetery at Syracuse, Mo. (Morgan county)	March 10, "		
38	2	3 miles north of Syracuse, Mo. (Near Evansville Church, Cooper county)	March 10, "		
39	1	Catholic Burying-ground, near Tipton, Mo.	March 10, "		
40	109	Fremont Burying-ground, ¼ mile north of Tipton, Moniteau county, Mo.	March 19, "		
41	1	Mr. McKee's farm, 12 miles north of Tipton, Mo.	March 19, "		
42	2	Grave-yard near Versailles, Morgan county, Mo.	March 19, "		
43	5	Cemetery at Waynesville, Mo. (Pulaski county)	April 3, "		
		Total removed to Jefferson Barracks		5,055	
1	38	City Cemetery at Boonville, Cooper county, Mo.	April 11, 1868.		Jefferson City National Cemetery, Mo. (Cole county.)
2	1	W. Jones' land, 3 miles south of Boonville, Mo.	April 11, "		
3	8	S. Mersteller's land, ¼ mile east of the eastern boundary line of the city of Boonville, Mo.	April 11, "		
4	1	H. A. Swauld's land, 4 miles southwest of Boonville, Mo.	April 11, "		
5	1	Brunswick, Chauton county, Mo. (Grave-yard ½ mile east of)	April 23, "		
6	2	Georgetown, Mo. (1 mile south of town, and 200 yards east of the old Georgetown road)	Feb'y 18, "		
7	2	E. O. Cheatham's land, 2 miles northwest of Georgetown, Mo.	Feb'y 18, "		
8	2	Wm. Gentry's land, ¾ mile southwest of Georgetown, Mo.	Feb'y 18, "		
9	1	J. S. Major's land, 2 miles northwest of Georgetown, Mo.	Feb'y 18, "		
		Carried forward		56	

Virginia, Alabama, Mississippi, Arkansas, Tennessee, Kentucky, and Missouri, to Tennessee.—Continued.

No.	Number of Graves.	NUMBER AND ORIGINAL LOCATION OF GRAVES. Original Location.	DATE OF REMOVAL OF BODIES.	FINAL DISPOSITION OF REMAINS. Number of Bodies.	Final Resting-place.
		Brought forward		56	
10	27	Montgomery Burying-ground, north side of Georgetown, Mo.	Feb'y 18, 1868.		
11	7	Spaden Burying-ground, south side of Georgetown, Mo.	Feb'y 18, "		
12	3	Mrs. Lucy Billingsly's land, 1¼ mile northeast of Glasgow, Mo.	April 21, "		
13	20	Washington Cemetery, ¼ mile east of the city of Glasgow, Howard county, Mo.	April 21, "		
14	78	Otterville Cemetery, Mo. (North side of town of Otterville)	March 3, "		
15	3	Otterville, Mo. (1 mile south of town, in Morgan county)	March 3, "		
16	13	Otterville, Mo. (1 mile east of town, in the old fortifications)	March 3, "		
17	1	Otterville, Mo. (1¼ mile east of town, east side of Lamine river)	March 3, "		
18	11	Mr. Hogan's farm, 3 miles west of Otterville, Mo.	March 3, "		
19	11	R. B. McMillan's farm, 2 miles southeast of Otterville, Mo.	March 3, "	232	Jefferson City National Cemetery, Mo. (Cole connty.)
20	61	Sedalia Cemetery, Sedalia, Pettis county, Mo.	Feb'y 18, "		
21	7	Smithton Cemetery, Smithton, Pettis county, Mo.	Feb'y 18, "		
		Total removed to Jefferson City		288	
1	221	Cassville Cemetery, Cassville, Barry county, Mo.	Jan'y 21, 1868.		
2	2	Camp Bliss, Barry county, Mo.	Jan'y 24, "		
3	3	Flat creek, Barry county, Mo.	Jan'y 23, "		
4	3	Judge Saunders, Christian county, Mo.	Feb'y 6, "		
5	4	Stevens' Mills, Christian county, Mo.	Feb'y 6, "		
6	144	Wilson's creek, Greene county, Mo.	Feb'y 6, "		
7	2	Coursey's Stage station, Laclede county, Mo. (27 miles from Springfield)	March 2, "	1,049	Springfield National Cemetery, Mo. (Greene county.)
8	57	Cemetery ¼ mile west of Lebanon, Laclede county, Mo.	Feb'y 27, "		
9	3	Mr. Apling's farm, Lebanon, Laclede county, Mo. (¼ mile north of public square)	Feb'y 27, "		
10	2	¼ mile east of Lebanon, Mo.	Feb'y 27, "		
11	2	Mr. Vernon's farm, 2 miles N. W. of public square, Lebanon, Mo.	Feb'y 27, "		

12	584	Springfield Cemetery, ¼ mile north of Court-house, Springfield, Mo.	Feb'y 22, 1868.		
13	15	Crane creek, Stone county, Mo.	Jan'y 30, "		
14	5	Dug Springs, Stone county, Mo.	Jan'y 31, "		
15	2	Sand Springs, Webster county, Mo. (20 miles from Springfield).	March 2, "		
		Total removed to Springfield.		1,049	
1	10	Within the limits of the present National Cemetery at Fort Scott, Kansas.			
2	15	Camp's 5-acre lot, at a point about 56 rods north of the north line of the National Cemetery at Fort Scott, Kansas.			
3	67	Old Military Cemetery, on west side of city of Fort Scott, Kansas.			
4	5	Fort Lincoln, Bourbon county, Kansas, at a point 100 yards north, on a road from John Knowles' house, thence east 25 yards.			
5	1	East bank of Little Osage creek and west of house of Thos. W. White.			Fort Scott National Cemetery, Kansas. (Bourbon county.)
6	13	Hayne's farm, ¼ mile northeast of Fort Scott, Kansas.	From May 20, 1867, to July 20, 1867.	121	
7	1	Turkey creek, Bourbon county, Kansas, on Judge Holt's farm.			
8	1	McNeal's farm, near Balltown, Vernon county, Mo.			
9	1	Young's farm, Shiloah creek, Bourbon county, Kansas.			
10	1	Prairie, 2 miles east of premises of W. Dennison, Little Dry Wood creek, Vernon county, Mo.			
11	1	Hogan's crossing, Dry Wood creek, Vernon county, Mo.			
12	1	150 yards from northeast corner of Gen'l Bailey's premises, Dry Wood, Vernon county, Mo.			
13	3	Smith's farm, on State line, Bourbon county, Kansas.			
14	1	On Morse's branch of Dry Wood creek, Dry Wood, Vernon county, Mo.			
		Total removed to Fort Scott.		121	
1	3	Within the limits of the present cemetery at Barnesville, Kansas.			
2	8	Camp Denver, on Indian creek, 2 miles N.E. of Barnesville, Kan.	From June 1, 1867, to June 17, 1867.	14	Barnesville Cemetery, Kansas (Bourbon county.)
3	1	South bank of Little Osage river, on east side of road from Barnesville to Fort Scott, Kansas.			
4	2	Burkholder's farm, on west bank of Little Osage river, 2 miles east of Barnesville, Kansas.			
		Total removed to Barnesville.		14	

No.	Number of Graves.	NUMBER AND ORIGINAL LOCATION OF GRAVES. Original Location.	DATE OF REMOVAL OF BODIES.	FINAL DISPOSITION OF REMAINS. Number of Bodies.	Final Resting-place.
1	1	Dooley's grave-yard, 5½ miles east of Ottumwa, Kansas	From April 23, 1867, to April 28, 1867.	3	Ottumwa Cemetery, Coffy county, Kan.
2	1	Bowen's grave-yard, Ottumwa, Kansas			
3	1	A point 2 yards S. of place of reinterment, Ottumwa Cemetery, Kan.			
		Total removed to Ottumwa		3	
1	2	Aubrey Cemetery, Johnson county, Kansas	From May 1,'67, to May 13, '67.	9	Olathe Cemetery, Johnson county, Kan.
2	7	Cemetery ¼ mile from Olathe, Kansas			
		Total removed to Olathe		9	
1	10	A point 60 yards southwest from place of reinterment	From May 18, 1867, to June 17, 1867.	30	Mound City Cemetery, Linn county, Kansas.
2	3	25 yards northwest from place of reinterment			
3	1	43 yards west of place of reinterment			
4	1	20 yards southwest of place of reinterment			
5	6	Mine creek battle-field, 5 miles northeast of Mound City, Linn county, Kansas			
6	4	Cemetery at Mapleton, Bourbon county, Kansas. (10 miles southwest of Mound City)			
7	2	Cemetery at Trading Post, 12 miles northeast of Mound City, Kan.			
8	1	Bank of Mine creek, 5 miles northeast of Mound City, Kansas, and near battle-field at Mine creek			
9	1	Bank of Mine creek, 8 miles easterly from Mound City, Kansas, near public road			
10	1	Saddler's crossing, Big Sugar creek, 12 miles northwest of Mound City, Kansas			
		Total removed to Mound City		30	

51

				Dates	No.	Destination
1	4	Within the limits of the present Cemetery, Iola, Kansas.	}	From May 14, 1867, to May 17, 1867.	6	Iola Cemetery, Allen county, Kansas.
2	1	Carlisle, Allen county, Kansas. (¾ mile north of Presbyterian Meeting-house).				
3	1	75 yards west of Carpenter's School-house, 5 miles north of Iola, Kansas.				
		Total removed to Iola			6	
1	11	At points from 32 to 127 yards from place of reinterment.	}	From June 5, 1867, to June 20, 1867.	17	Paola Cemetery, Miami county, Kansas.
2	4	Camp Coldwater Grove, Miami county, Kansas. (15 miles east of Paola)				
3	2	Rockville, Miami county, Kansas				
		Total removed to Paola			17	
1	2	Within the limits of the present Cemetery, Geneva, Kansas	}		3	Geneva Cemetery, Allen county, Kan.
2	1	Neosho Falls, Woodson county, Kansas				
		Total removed to Geneva			3	
1	1	Abandoned Cemetery, 2 miles northwesterly from Louisville, Pottawattamie county, Kansas			1	New Cemetery, Louisville, Pottawattamie county, Kansas.
		Total removed to New Cemetery			1	

ALPHABETICAL INDEX

TO

ORIGINAL PLACES OF BURIAL, WHENCE BODIES HAVE BEEN REMOVED.

Name of Locality.	Page.	Name of Locality.	Page.
Abbeville, Ga.	25	Bourbon county, Kans.	50
Abbeville, Miss.	30	Bowling Green, Ky.	45
Aberdeen, Miss.	30	Bradyville, Tenn.	41
Abingdon, Va.	37	Branchville, Tenn.	41
Adkin's Switch, Va.	37	Brandy Station, Va.	12
Albany, Ga.	25	Brashear, La.	33
Alexandria, Tenn.	40	Brice's X Roads, Miss.	30
Allen county, Kans.	51	Bridgewater, Va.	17
Americus, Ga.	25	Bristoe Station, Va.	9
Andersonville, Ga.	25	Bristol, Tenn.	37
Antietam, Md.	8	Britton's Lano, Tenn.	30
Arsenal, U. S., Fla.	27	Brownsville, Md.	8
Ashton Mill, Tenn.	40	Brownsville, Tenn.	39
Athens, Ala.	30–32–40	Brunswick, Mo.	47
Aubrey, Kans.	50–41	Bull Run, Va.	9
Auburn, Va.	9	Bull's Gap, Tenn.	37
Augusta county, Va.	17	Burkesville, Ky.	45
		Burkettsville, Md.	8
Bainbridge, Ga.	25	Burnsville, Miss.	30
Baldwin, Miss.	30		
Balltown, Mo.	49	Camden, Ark.	33
Barbour's X Roads, Va.	9	Campbell Station, Tenn.	37
Barboursville, Ky.	37–44	Campbellville, Ky.	43
Bardstown, Ky.	43	Camp Bliss, Mo.	48
Barnesville, Kans.	49	Camp Coldwater, Kans.	51
Barry Ford, Va.	12	Camp Davis, Miss.	30
Barry county, Mo.	48	Camp Denver, Kans.	49
Barton Station, Ala.	30	Camp Nelson, Ky.	42
Baton Rouge, La.	32–33	Camp Pitman, Ky.	44
Bayou Bœuf, La.	33	Camp Stevens, La.	33
Bayou Sara, La.	35	Camp Wickliffe, Ky.	43
Bealton, Va.	9	Cane Valley, Ky.	43
Bealton Station, Va.	9	Canton, Miss.	30
Bean Station, Tenn.	37	Carlisle, Kans.	51
Bell Buckle, Tenn.	41	Carter's Station, Tenn.	37–41
Berlin, Md.	8	Casey's creek, Ky.	43
Bethel, Tenn.	30	Cassville, Mo.	48
Bethel, Ky.	43	Catlett Station, Va.	9
Beverly Ford, Va.	9	Cavetown, Md.	8
Big Creek Gap, Tenn.	37	Cedar Creek bridge, Va.	24–21
Big Hill, Ky.	44	Cedar Mountain, Va.	18
Black Fish lake, Miss.	39	Centre Point, Ky.	45
Blackwell, Va.	9	Centreville, Ky.	45
Bloomington, Md.	8	Chacahoula, La.	33
Blountville, Tenn.	37	Chauton county, Mo.	47
Blue Springs, Tenn.	37	Charles City, Va.	13
Bolivar, Tenn.	30	Cheneyville, La.	37
Bolivar, Va.	22	Cherokee Station, Ala.	30
Boonesboro', Md.	8	Chewalla, Tenn.	31
Boonville, Mo.	47	Chickasaw Bayou, Miss.	28
Bonnet Carre, La.	33	Christian county, Mo.	48
Boston, Ky.	44	Christiansburg, Va.	17

Name of Locality.	Page.	Name of Locality.	Page.
Cipple creek, Tenn	41	Fayetteville, Tenn	41
Clandestine House, Ark	39	Fisherville, Tenn	39
Clark county, Va	21	Flat creek, Mo	48
Claryville, Md	8	Flat Lick, Ky	38
Clear creek, Tenn	38	Fontania, La	36
Clear creek, La	37	Fort Curtis, Ark	39
Clear Spring, Md	8	Fort DeRussey, La	37
Clinton, Ga	25	Fort Hill, Miss	28
Clinton, Tenn	38	Fort Hindman, Ark	39
Clinton, La	36	Fort Lincoln, Kans	49
Cloyd's Mountain, Va	17	Fort Macomb, La	33
Coffeeville, Miss	31	Fort Pendleton, Md	8
Coldwater river, Miss	39	Fort Pickering, Tenn	39
Collierville, Tenn	39	Fort Pike, La	33
Columbia, Tenn	41	Fort Pillow, Tenn	39
Columbia, Ky	45	Fort Rosecrans, Tenn	41
Columbus, Ga	25	Fort Scott, Kans	49
Columbus, Miss	31	Four-mile bridge, Miss	28
Columbus, Tenn	38	Franklin, La	33
Cool Spring, Va	21	Franklin, Va	18
Cooper county, Mo	47	Franklin, Tenn	41
Concord, Tenn	38	Franklin, Mo.	46
Connor's Store, Va	17	Frederick, Md	8
Corinth, Miss	31	Frederick county, Va	21–22
Coursey's Station, Mo	48	Fredericktown, Ky	43
Courtland, Ala	31	Freeman's Ford, Va	10
Covington, Va	17	Fremont, Mo	47
Covington, Ga	25	Frostburg, Md	8
Cowan, Tenn	41	Fulbright Springs, Mo	47
Cross Keys, Va	17	Fulton county, Penn	8
Crab Orchard, Ky	43	Funkstown, Md	8
Crane creek, Mo	49	Furrey's Furnace, Va	17
Culpeper, Va	13		
Cumberland, Md	8	Gainesville, Va	10
Cumberland Ford, Ky	38	Gauley, Va	18
Cumberland Gap, Tenn	38	Geneva, Kans	51
Cuthbert, Ga	25	Glasgow, Ky	45
		Glasgow, Mo	48
Dandridge, Tenn	38	Glendale, Miss	31
Decatur, Ala	31	Georgetown, Mo	47–48
Decherd, Tenn	41	Georgetown, Va	10
Dent county, Mo	46	Goodrich's Landing, La	28
De Soto, La	28	Goose creek, Tenn	38
Dixon Station, Ala	31	Gordon, Ga	25
Donaldsville, La	33	Gordonsville, Va	15
Dry creek, Va	17	Grand Junction, Tenn	31
Dry Wood, Mo	49	Greene county, Mo	48
Dublin, Va	38	Green River bridge, Ky	43
Duckport, La	28	Greensburg, Ky	43
Dug Springs, Mo	49	Greenville, Tenn	38
Dunlap Springs, Miss	31	Griswoldville, Ga	25
Dyer's Station, Tenn	31	Gun Spring, Tenn	41
Eatenton, Ga	25–26	Hackman, Tenn	39
Egypt Station, Miss	31	Hagerstown, Md	8
Elkmont, Ala	31	Hall's Ferry, Miss	28
Elk river, Tenn	41	Hamburg, Tenn	31
Ellistown, Miss	31	Hancock, Md	8
Elmwood, Tenn	39	Hannibal, Mo	46
Estell Spring, Tenn	41	Harding House, Tenn	41
Evansville, Mo	47	Harper's Ferry, Va	22
		Harrisonburg, Va	18
Farmington, Tenn	31–41	Harris Station, Ala	31
Fayette C. H., Va	18	Hatchie river, Miss	31

Name of Locality.	Page.	Name of Locality.	Page.
Hawk House, Ark	39	Liberty, Ky	43
Hawkinsville, Ga	25	Liberty, Va	10
Helena, Ark	39	Liberty Gap, Tenn	41
Henry and Emery College, Va	38	Liberty Mills, Va	15
Hickory Hill, Tenn	41	Lick creek, Tenn	38
Highland county, Va	19	Licking, Mo	46
Hillsboro', Ga	25	Limestone, Tenn	38
Hillsboro', Tenn	41	Linn county, Kans	50
Hogan's Crossing, Mo	49	Little Orleans, Md	8
Holly Springs, Miss	31	Locust Spring, Md	8
Hoover's Gap, Tenn	41	London, Ky	44–45
Houston, Mo	46	London, Tenn	38
Howard county, Mo	48	Loudon county, Va	22
Humboldt, Tenn	31–39	Louisville, Tenn	38
		Louisville, Kans	51
Indianola, Tex	37	Luray, Va	19
Iola, Kans	51		
Ironton, Mo	46	Macon, Ga	25–26
Irving's X Roads, Ga	25	Madison C. H., Va	15
Irwinton, Ga	25	Madisonville, Tenn	38
Island No. 10	39	Manassas Station, Va	10
Island No. 40	39	Manchester, Tenn	41
Isler Landing, Tenn	39	Manchester, Ky	45
Iuka, Miss	31	Manny's Grove, Tenn	41
		Mapleton, Kans	50
Jacinto, Miss	31	Marion, Va	38
Jacksboro', Tenn	38	Martinsburg, W. Va	10
Jackson, La	34–35–36	Maryland Heights, Md	8
Jackson, Tenn	31	Mason Station, Tenn	40
Jackson River depot, Va	18	Maynardsville, Tenn	38
Jefferson county, Va	22	McDonough, Ga	26
Job's House, Miss	31	McMinnville, Tenn	41
Johnson county, Kans	50	Meadow Bluff, Va	19
Johnson's depot, Tenn	38	Meadow Station, Tenn	31
Jonesboro', Tenn	38	Meeting House, Ky	44
Jonesboro', Ala	31	Memphis, Tenn	40
Jonesville, Va	38	Miami county, Kans	51
		Middlebury Station, Tenn	31
Keedysville, Md	8	Middletown, Va	21–22
Kelly's Ford, Va	10–15	Middletown, Md	8
Kenton, Tenn	31	Miffin, Tenn	31
Kernstown, Va	21	Milford, Va	19
Kingston, Tenn	38	Milledgeville, Ga	26
Knoxville, Tenn	38	Milliken's Bend, La	28–29
Kossuth, Miss	31	Mine creek, Kans	50
		Mitchell's Station. Va	15
Labadieville, La	33	Moniteau county, Mo	47
Lacey Springs, Va	19	Monocacy Junction, Md	8
Laclede county, Mo	48	Monterey, Va	19
Lacopolis, Miss	39	Monticello, Ga	26
Lafayette, Tenn	40	Morgan county, Mo	47–48
Lafourche Crossing, La	33	Morganza, La	36
Lafourche Parish, La	33	Morristown, Tenn	38
La Grange, Tenn	40	Morrisville, Va	10–15
Lake Springs, Mo	46	Moscow, Tenn	40
Lancaster, Ky	42	Moselle Station, Mo	46
Lavergue, Tenn	41	Mossy creek, Tenn	38
Lebanon, Ky	43	Mound City, Kans	50
Lebanon, Tenn	41	Mount Airy, Va	39
Lebanon, Mo	48	Mount Holly, Va	10
Leighton, Ala	31	Mount Pleasant, La	35–36
Lenoir's Station, Tenn	38	Mount Pleasant, Tenn	40
Lewisburg, Va	18	Mount Pleasant Landing, La	36
Lexington, Tenn	31	Mount Solon, Va	19

Name of Locality.	Page.	Name of Locality.	Page.
Mount Vernon, Tenn	40	Rienzi, Miss	32
Mount Vernon, Ky	45	Rockingham county, Va	20
Murfreesboro', Tenn	41	Rockville, Kans	51
		Rolla, Mo	47
Natchez, Miss	28	Rondleson, La	35
Neatsville, Ky	43	Russellville, Tenn	39
Neosho Falls, Kans	51	Rutherford's Station, Tenn	32
New Baltimore, Va	10	Rutledge, Tenn	39
New Haven, Ky	44		
New Madrid, Mo	40	Saddler's Crossing, Kans	50
New Market, Va	10–23	Saint Francisville, La	34
New Market, Tenn	39	Saint James' College, Md	9
New Market, Ky	44	Saint Louis, Mo	47
New River bridge, Va	39	Saint Mary's Parish, La	33
Nicholasville, Ky	42	Salem, Miss	32
Noakesville, Va	10	Salem, Mo	47
Normandy, Tenn	41	Salem, Va	11–20
		Saltillo, Miss	32
Oakland, Md	8	Saltville, Va	39
Oakland, Va	18	Sandersville, Ga	26–27
Okolona, Miss	31	Sand Springs, Mo	49
Olathe, Kans	50	Sandy Hook, Md	8
Oldtown, Md	8	Saulsbury, Tenn	32
Olive Branch, La	34	Scull Camp bridge, Tenn	42
Omega Landing, La	29	Sedalia, Mo	48
Orange C. H., Va	15	Sevierville, Tenn	39
Orleans, Va	10	Sharpsburg, Md	8
Osceola, Mo	40	Shelbyville, Tenn	42
Otterville, Mo	48	Shenandoah county, Va	22–23–24
Ottumwa, Kans	50	Shepard Mountain, Mo	46
Oxford, Miss	32	Shiloah creek, Kans	49
		Silver Spring, Tenn	42
Page county, Va	19	Sinking creek, Ky	39
Paris, Tenn	40	Smithton, Mo	48
Parker's X Roads, Tenn	32	Smoketown, Md	8
Paw Paw Island, La	29	Snicker's Ferry, Va	21
Pensacola, Fla	27	Snyder's Bluff, Miss	29
Pettis county, Mo	48	South Mountain, Md	8
Phelps county, Mo	47	Sparta, Tenn	42
Piedmont, W. Va	10–19	Sperryville, Va	15
Pinson Station, Tenn	32	Springfield, Mo	47–49
Pittsburg Landing, Tenn	32	Spring Hill, Tenn	42
Plaquemine, La	33	Sprout Spring, Miss	29
Pleasant Hill, Ky	45	Stanford, Ky	43
Pocahontas, Tenn	32	Stanfordsville, Ga	27
Point of Rocks, Md	8	Staunton, Va	20
Point Pleasant, Mo	40	Stevensburg, Va	15
Pollard, Ala	27	Stevens' Mills, Mo	48
Poor Valley Ridge, Ky	39	Stone county, Mo	49
Port Hudson, La	34–35–36	Stone's river, Tenn	42
Port Republic, Va	19–20	Strawberry Plains, Tenn	39
Pottawattamie county, Kans	51	Sudley Mills, Va	11
Pulaski, Tenn	42	Sunshine, Ga	26
Pulaski county, Mo	47	Syracuse, Mo	47
Purdy, Tenn	32		
		Tazewell, Tenn	39
Raccoon Ford, Va	15	Tennville Station, Ga	27
Rapidan Ford, Va	15	Terrebonne Parish, La	33
Rapidan Station, Va	15	Terrebonne Station, La	33
Rappahannock Station, Va	10–15	Texas county, Mo	46
Ration Hill, Miss	·29	Thibodeaux, La	34
Readyville, Tenn	42	Thomasville, Ga	27
Rectortown, Va	11	Thompson House, Ark	40
Rheatown, Tenn	39	Thompson's Station, Tenn	42

Name of Locality.	Page.	Name of Locality.	Page.
Thoroughfare Gap, Va	11	Wartrace, Tenn	42
Tigersville Station, La	34	Washington C. H., Va	16
Tompkinsville, Ky	45–46	Waterloo, Va	12
Toomsboro', Ga	27	Water Valley, Miss	32
Tipton, Mo	47	Waynesville, Mo	47
Tiptonville, Tenn	40	Weaversville, Va	12
Trading Post, Kans	50	Weverton, Md	9
Trenton, Tenn	32	Webster county, Mo	49
Trevilian Station, Va	16	Westernport, Md	9
Troy, Tenn	32	West Point, Miss	32
Tullahoma, Tenn	42	White Cat, Ky	45
Tupello, Miss	32	White House, Miss	30
Turkey creek, Kans	49	White Plains, Va	12
Tuscumbia, Ala	32	White Springs, Va	39
Two-mile bridge, Miss	29	White Sulphur Springs, Va	20
		Williamsburg, Ky	45
Union City, Tenn	32	Williamsport, Md	9
Union Depot, Tenn	40	Wilson's creek, Mo	48
Union Mills, Va	11	Wilson's Landing, La	37
Urbanna, Md	9	Winchester, Va	21
		Winchester, Tenn	42
Vandalia, Miss	28	Wolf river, Tenn	40
Vernon county, Mo	49	Wolf River bridge, Tenn	40
Versailles, Mo	47	Woodbury, Tenn	42
Vicksburg, Miss	28–29–30	Woodson county, Kans	51
Victoria, Tex	37	Woodville, Va	17
		Worthville, Ga	27
Wade's Station, Va	21	Wyatt, Miss	40
Walker's Ford, Tenn	39	Wytheville, Va	39
Warren county, Va	24		
Warrenton, Va	11	Yellow Bayou, La	37
Warrenton Junction, Va	11	Young's Point, La	30
Warrington Springs, Va	11		

ALPHABETICAL INDEX

TO

NATIONAL CEMETERIES WHERE BODIES HAVE BEEN DEPOSITED.

	PAGE.		PAGE.
Alexandria, La	37	Lebanon, Ky	43
Andersonville, Ga	25	London, Ky	44
Antietam, Md	8	Louisville, Kans	51
Arlington, Va	9		
		Memphis, Tenn	39
Barancas, Fla	27	Mobile, Ala	27
Barnesville, Kans	49	Mound City, Kans	50
Baton Rouge, La	33		
Brownsville, Texas	37	Natchez, Miss	28
Camp Nelson, Ky	42	Olathe, Kans	50
Chalmette, La	33	Ottumwa, Kans	50
Corinth, Miss	31		
Culpeper, Va	13	Paola, Kans	51
		Port Hudson, La	35
Fort Scott, Kans	49		
		Springfield, Mo	48
Geneva, Kans	51	Staunton, Va	17
		Stone's river, Tenn	41
Iola, Kans	51		
		Tompkinsville, Ky	45
Jefferson Barracks, Mo	47		
Jefferson City, Mo	47	Vicksburg, Miss	29
Knoxville, Tenn	37	Winchester, Va	21

Quartermaster General's Office, General Orders No. 33, Aug. 13, 1868.

STATEMENT

OF THE

DISPOSITION OF SOME OF THE BODIES

OF

DECEASED UNION SOLDIERS

AND

PRISONERS OF WAR

WHOSE REMAINS HAVE BEEN REMOVED

TO

NATIONAL CEMETERIES

IN THE SOUTHERN AND WESTERN STATES.

VOLUME III.

Life's tumultuous battles o'er,'
O, how sweetly sleep the brave!

WASHINGTON:
GOVERNMENT PRINTING OFFICE.
1868.

STATEMENT OF FINAL DISPOSITION
OF SOLDIERS' REMAINS, VOL. III.

GENERAL ORDERS } QUARTERMASTER GENERAL'S OFFICE,
No. 33. } WASHINGTON, D. C., *Aug.* 13, 1868.

The following "Statement of the disposition of some of the bodies of deceased Union Soldiers and Prisoners of War, whose remains have been removed to National Cemeteries in the Southern and Western States," (being the third volume of the same,) prepared in the Cemeterial branch of this office, under the direction of Brevet Brigadier General ALEXANDER J. PERRY, Q. M., U. S. Army, is published by authority of the Secretary of War, for the information of surviving comrades and friends, and for use in connection with the "Rolls of Honor" heretofore published by this Office.

M. C. MEIGS,
Quartermaster General,
Brevet Major General, U. S. Army.

QUARTERMASTER GENERAL'S OFFICE,
WASHINGTON, D. C., *Aug.* 13, 1868.

Brevet Major General M. C. MEIGS,
Quartermaster General,
U. S. Army,

GENERAL:

The enclosed "Statement of the *Final Disposition* of the Bodies of Deceased Union Soldiers and Prisoners of War, whose remains have been removed to National Cemeteries in the Southern and Western States," prepared in this Office by Brevet Colonel C. W. FOLSOM, A. Q. M., U. S. Vols., is respectfully transmitted to you, with the request that it be printed and distributed for use in connection with the "Rolls of Honor" heretofore issued from this Office.

I am, General, very respectfully,
Your obedient servant,
ALEX. J. PERRY,
Bvt. Brig. General and Q. M., U. S. A.

QUARTERMASTER GENERAL'S OFFICE,
CEMETERIAL BRANCH,
WASHINGTON, D. C., *July* 29, 1868.

Brevet Brig. General A. J. PERRY,
Quartermaster, U. S. Army,
Q. M. General's Office, Washington, D. C.

GENERAL:

I have the honor to transmit herewith for publication, in connection with the "Rolls of Honor" which are published by the Quartermaster General, a third volume of "Statements of Final Disposition of the Bodies of Deceased Union Soldiers and Prisoners of War in the National Cemeteries in the Southern and Western States."

This volume contains, among others, the principal removals to the National Cemeteries at Alexandria, La., Brownsville, Tex., Louisville, Ky., New Orleans, La., Fort Donelson, Tenn., Jefferson Barracks, Mo., Nashville, Tenn., Salisbury, N. C., Shiloh, Tenn., and Springfield, Mo.; also additional removals to Andersonville, Ga., Galveston, Tex., Lawton, Ga., and Marietta, Ga.

Thus the removal of 35,577 bodies of deceased Union Soldiers and Prisoners of War, (as shown in this Statement,) has been made from 314 different localities, scattered throughout the Southern and Western States, to 21 of the established National Cemeteries.

The work of removals has necessarily been suspended during the hot season in the more Southern localities, owing to the extreme heat, and for the preservation of the public health; but it will be resumed in the autumn, and, it is thought, will be completed during the year 1868.

Doubtless many graves have not yet been found, although the search for them has been diligent; but by the co-operation of the friends and comrades of those soldiers who died and were buried on remote skirmish fields, or in isolated spots, it is hoped that the Government will yet be able to discover the resting place of many who are, as yet, unfound. To this end, any information concerning the burial place of Union Soldiers, in isolated or scattered localities, is earnestly solicited; which information may be forwarded to the Quartermaster General, U. S. Army, at Washington, D. C., free of postage.

It is thought that this Statement will furnish valuable material for future records, and afford some assistance in identifying a great number of those whose graves now bear only the sad inscription, "Unknown."

Similar Statements will be prepared from time to time, as the necessary information is received in this Office, thus finally furnishing a complete record of all such removals and reinterments of the remains of deceased Union Soldiers.

    I am, General, very respectfully,
      Your obedient servant,
        C. W. FOLSOM,
        Bvt. Colonel, A. Q. M., U. S. Vols.

TABLE OF CONTENTS.

List of the States from and to which the Bodies of Deceased Union Soldiers and Prisoners of War have been removed.

No.	From places in—	To Cemeteries in—	Page.
I.	North Carolina	N. Carolina	8
II.	Georgia and Alabama	Georgia	8
III.	Arkansas	Arkansas	12
IV.	Louisiana	Louisiana	13
V.	Texas	Texas	15
VI.	Tennessee, Kentucky, Mississippi, and Alabama	Tennessee	16
VII.	Kentucky	Kentucky	23
VIII.	Michigan	Michigan	30
IX.	Missouri and Arkansas	Missouri	30
X.	Montana Territory	Montana Ter.	34
	Alphabetical Index of places from which bodies have been removed		35
	Alphabetical Index of Cemeteries to which bodies have been removed		38

I.—From North Carolina to North Carolina.

No.	Number and Original Location of Graves.		Date of Removal of Bodies.	Final Disposition of Remains.	
	Number of Graves.	Original Location.		Number of Bodies.	Final Resting-place.
1	57	Camp York, N. C. (7 miles west of Salisbury)			
2	71	Charlotte, N. C.			
3	12	Lexington, N. C.			
4	64	Salisbury, N. C. (Within the limits of the present National Cemetery)			Salisbury National Cemetery, N. C. (Rowan county.)
5	90	Near Salisbury, N. C. (300 yards northeast of Cemetery, by the side of ravine)		412	
6	93	Lutheran grave-yard, Salisbury, N. C.			
7	2	English Church-yard, near Salisbury, N. C.			
8	5	Gold Hill road, 1 mile from Salisbury, N. C.			
9	4	Bank of the Yadkin, N. C.			
10	8	On N. C. Railroad, 1¼ mile west of Salisbury, N. C.			
11	1	Mrs. Johnson's garden, Salisbury, N. C.			
		Total removed to Salisbury		412	

II.—From Georgia and Alabama to Georgia.

No.	Number of Graves.	Original Location.	Date of Removal of Bodies.	Number of Bodies.	Final Resting-place.
1	2	Wm. Flander's place, 18 miles south of Bartow, Ga.			
2	1	Thos. Harris' land, 3 miles southwest of Davidsboro', Ga.			
3	1	Hawkinsville, Pulaski county, Ga. (West bank Oomulgee river).			
4	1	T. S. Barton's farm, 1¼ mile north of Station No. 9½, C. R. R., Ga.	Since March 19, 1868.	14	Andersonville National Cemetery, Ga. (Elbert county.)
5	1	Mrs. Lambert's place, ¼ mile north of Station No. 9½, C. R. R., Ga.			
6	1	Mr. Bowrick's place, Washington county, Ga.			
7	2	Wm. Flander's place, Washington county, Ga.			
8	1	S. Jackson's place, Washington county, Ga.			
9	1	B. Hall's place, Washington county, Ga.			
10	1	Irving Jackson's land, Washington county, Ga.			

11	1	B. Hall's plantation, 25 yards from Sandersville and Louisville road, Ga.		14
12	1	Mr. Bowick's place, Democrat road, Ga. (Under a pine tree)		
		Total removed to Andersonville		
				Atlanta and Marietta Nat'l Cem'y, Ga. (Fulton county.)
1	12	Marietta, Ga.	Feb'y, 1867	
2	607	Around Marietta, Ga.	Jan. and Feb., '67	
3	23	Atlanta, Ga.	May to Oct., '67	
4	278	Near Atlanta, Ga.	Feb., March, and May, 1867	
5	800	East of Atlanta, Ga.	May to Oct., '67	
6	309	West of Atlanta, Ga.	Aug. & Sept., '67	
7	4	North of Atlanta, Ga.	Nov., 1867	
8	60	Southwest of Atlanta, Ga.	Sept. & Oct., '67	
9	50	Southeast of Atlanta, Ga.	Nov., 1867	
10	774	Around Kenesaw, Ga.	Feb. to May, '67	
11	35	Dallas and vicinity, Ga.	May and Oct., '67	
12	480	New Hope Church, Ga.	Jan. to June, '67	
13	180	Peachtree creek, Ga.	Jan., Feb., and March, 1867	
14	9	Resaca, Ga.	June and Oct., '67	
15	110	Rome, Ga.	Jan. and Feb., '67	
16	198	Around Big Shanty, Ga.	May to Sept., '67	
17	59	Cartersville, Ga.	Jan., 1867	
18	10	Coosa river, Ga.	Feb., 1867	
19	295	Allatoona, Ga.	Feb. and Mar., '67	
20	221	Near Pine mountain, Ga.	Feb., Mar., and April, 1867	
21	30	Calhoun, Ga.	March, 1867	
22	2	Athens City Cemetery, Ga.	May, 1867	
23	105	Acworth, Ga.	May and Oct., '67	
24	62	Hospital Cemetery, near Poor-house place, N.W. of Atlanta, Ga.	May, 1867	
25	92	Eutoy creek, near Ezra Church, Ga.	May, 1867	
26	11	Polk county, Ala.	May, 1867	
27	142	Near Vining's Station, Ga.	May, 1867	
28	111	Peachtree Creek road, Ga.	May, 1867	
29	389	Jonesboro' Battle-field, Ga.	May to Dec., '67	
30	1	Cedartown, Ga.	June, 1867	
		Carried forward		5,459
				5 459

From Georgia and Alabama to Georgia—Continued.

No.	Number of Graves.	NUMBER AND ORIGINAL LOCATION OF GRAVES. Original Location.	DATE OF REMOVAL OF BODIES.	FINAL DISPOSITION OF REMAINS. Number of Bodies.	Final Resting-place.
		Brought forward		5,459	
31	2	Carrollton and Franklin road, Ga.	June, 1867		
32	1	Campbell county, Ga.	June, "		
33	14	Vicinity of Corinth road, Ga.	June, "		
34	2	Roswell, Ga.	June, "		
35	218	Near Chattahoochie river, Ga.	June & Aug., '67.		
36	20	Around Newnan, Ga.	July, 1867		
37	12	Gainesville, Ga.	July, 1867		
38	4	Dahlonega, Ga.	July and Oct.,'67.		Atlanta and Marietta Nat'l Cem'y, Ga. (Fulton county.)
39	7	Carroll county, Ga.	Aug., 1867		
40	15	Cherokee county, Ala.	Aug., "	658	
41	24	Decatur and vicinity, Ga.	Aug., "		
42	85	Lovejoy Station, Ga.	Aug., "		
43	4	Floyd county, Ga.	Sept., "		
44	25	Vicinity of East Point, Ga.	Sept., "		
45	5	Bear Creek Station, Ga.	Sept., "		
46	18	Fayette county, Ga.	Sept., "		
47	5	Rough and Ready Station, Ga.	Sept., "		
48	17	Vicinity of Stone mountain, Ga.	Sept., and Oct., 1867.		
49	3	De Kalb county, Ala.	Oct., 1867		
50	1	Chatooga, Ala.	Oct., "		
51	1	Wills' valley, on Lebanon and Judson road, Ala.	Oct., "		
52	4	Haralson county, Ga.	Oct., "		
53	1	Around Lost mountain, Ga.	Oct., "		
54	70	Augusta city, Ga.	Oct., "		
55	93	Around Augusta, Ga.	Nov., "		
56	7	Near Washington, Ga.	Dec., "		
		Total removed to Atlanta and Marietta		6,117	

1	2	Alexander, Ga. (Near Methodist Church)		
2	1	Near Alexander, Ga. (East of J. Sapp's house)		
3	4	Near Big Buckhead Church, Ga. (Trench south of small stream)		
4	1	A. Murphy's field, near Big Buckhead bridge, Ga.		
5	1	Cates' farm, Catesville, Ga.		
6	3	Mrs. Bragg's farm, 10 miles southeast of Lawton, Ga.		
7	492	Hack's Mills, near Lawton, Ga.		
8	2	West of Hack's Mills, near Lawton, Ga.		
9	2	Hargrave's farm, 8 miles northeast of Lawton, Ga.		
10	2	South side of Mrs. Jones' burnt house, near Lawton, Ga.		
11	193	Near Mrs. Jones' mill pond, near Lawton, Ga.		
12	1	Mat. Reynold's farm, 12 miles northeast of Lawton, Ga.		
13	2	H. Sussee's farm, 15 mil∴s southeast of Lawton, Ga.	Embraced in Vol. I. No dates given.	748	Lawton National Cemetery, Ga. (Clinch county.) [Afterwards removed to Beaufort, S.C.]
14	1	E. Scouger's farm, 25 miles northwest of Lawton, Ga.		
15	2	Stockade, (north side) near Lawton, Ga.		
16	1	Wadley's farm, 8 miles southeast of Lawton, Ga.		
17	1	Merryfield, Ga. (Near Louisville and Big Buckhead road)		
18	1	Chaplain's farm, near Millen, Ga.		
19	1	Thomas' Station, Ga. (East of station, near old church)		
20	3	Near Thomas' Station, Ga. (In a lane leading to Buckhead Church)		
21	2	Bell's farm, near Thomas' Station, Ga.		
22	3	Waynesboro' Cemetery, Ga.		
23	2	On Waynesboro' road, Ga. (Near crossing of Louisville and Big Buckhead road)		
24	2	Alexander road, near Waynesboro', Ga.		
25	1	Maj. Bennett's farm, Waynesboro' vicinity, Ga.		
26	2	Buckhead road, near Waynesboro', Ga.		
27	1	Near Dr. Carter's house, Waynesboro', Ga.		
28	6	Mrs. Corker's place, Waynesboro' and Big Buckhead road, Ga.		
29	2	Mrs. Holtmes' farm, near Waynesboro', Ga.		
30	1	Mrs. Jones' and Mrs. Carter's farms, near Waynesboro', Ga.		
31	1	Mr. McCuller's yard, on Waynesboro' and Big Buckhead road, Ga.		
32	1	R. Scales' family cemetery, Waynesboro' vicinity, Ga.		
33	1	Mrs. Sturgiss' house, Waynesboro', Ga.		
34	1	Thomas' farm, Waynesboro' vicinity, Ga.		
35	1	North of Tillas' store, near Waynesboro', Ga.		
36	3	J. B. Jones' farm, near old No. 9 Station, C. R. R.		
37	2	Wood's farm, north of Station No. 7, C. R. R.		
		Total removed to Lawton		748

III.—From Arkansas to Arkansas.

No.	Number of Graves.	NUMBER AND ORIGINAL LOCATION OF GRAVES. Original Location.	DATE OF REMOVAL OF BODIES.	FINAL DISPOSITION OF REMAINS.	
				Number of Bodies.	Final Resting-place.
1	23	Clarksville, Ark. (Civil Cemetery)			
2	2	Clarksville, Ark. (South of old mill, by 3 elm trees)			
3	1	Clarksville, Ark. (Top of hill, east of town)			
4	3	Boland's land, near Clarksville, Ark. (On side of hill, 300 yards from road)			
5	2	Boland's place, near Clarksville, Ark. (In cotton field, left of creek)			
6	1	Colored grave-yard, east of Clarksville, Ark.			
7	1	Davis' land, 4 miles from Clarksville, Ark.			
8	4	Heartgreave's land, Horse Head creek, 10 miles from Clarksville, Ark.	From March 18 to April 18, 1868.	69	Fort Smith National Cemetery, Ark. (Sebastian county.)
9	1	McGlaglin's land, near Clarksville, Ark. (¼ mile from cotton gin, and 500 yards from road)			
10	1	Nixe's place, near Clarksville, Ark. (Back of blacksmith shop, 20 yards from road)			
11	2	Nixe's place, near Clarksville, Ark. (In lane, ¼ mile below house)			
12	1	In woods, 19 miles from Clarksville, Ark. (200 yards from Boland's cottage, and 20 steps from road)			
13	1	More's land, 6 miles from Van Buren, Ark. (¼ mile from Smith's mill)			
14	1	Black Jack ridge, 1 mile from Smith, Scott county, Ark.	Month of May, 1868.		
15	2	Near Came hill, Sebastian county, Ark.			
16	4	Poteau mountain, Ark. (5 miles from the creek)			
17	1	Side of Porteau mountain, Ark. (4 miles from the creek)			
18	1	Silver creek, near Waldon, Ark.			
19	1	10 miles from Smith, Ark. (East side of Ganter's prairie)			
20	4	Tate's mill, on Dutches' creek, Ark.			
21	1	1 mile west of Waldon, Ark.			
22	2	Waldon, Scott county, Ark.			

13

23	7	1 mile east of Waldon, Ark. (In a family grave-yard)			
24	2	Scott county, Ark. (In the woods)			
		Total removed to Fort Smith		69	

IV.—From Louisiana to Louisiana.

1	2	Cloutierville, La.	May 4, 1868.		
2	1	Cotile Landing, La.	May 4, "		
3	27	Grand Ecore, La.	Apr. 28, "		
4	73	Mansfield, La. (City Cemetery)	April, "		
5	116	Mansfield, La. (Cross Roads Battle-field)	April, "		
6	11	Mott's Ferry, La.	May 4, "		
7	5	Natchitoches, La.	Apr. 28, "		
8	209	Pleasant Hill, La. (Battle-field)	April, "		
9	76	Shreveport, La. (National Cemetery)	March, "		
10	2	Joseph McEvry's field, La.	Apr. 22, "		
		Total removed to Alexandria		522	Alexandria National Cemetery, La. (Rapides county.)
1	4	Dr. Rhode's plantation, 3 miles north of Berwick, La.	April, 1868		
2	2	Mr. Smith's plantation, 5 miles north of Berwick, La.	April, "		
3	1	P. C. Bethell's plantation, left bank of Bayou Teche, 3¼ miles north of Franklin, La.	April, "		
4	1	L. Harding's plantation, 3 miles north of Franklin, La.	April, "		
5	4	J. D. Gidney's plantation, 3½ miles north of Grand Coteau, La. (Parish of St. Landry)	May, "		
6	3	Madame Gilboux's plantation, 4 miles north of Grand Coteau, La.	May, "		
7	16	D. W. Gladon's plantation, 3¼ miles north of Grand Coteau, La.	May, "		
8	4	McDowell's plantation, 2¼ miles south of Grand Coteau, La.	May, "		
9	14	Ex-Gov. Mouton's plantation, 4 miles southeast of Grand Coteau, La.	May, "		
10	1	Mr. Bayard's plantation, 2½ miles southeast of New Iberia, La. (Parish of St. Martin)	April, "		
11	1	T. J. Bronson's plantation, 8 miles south of New Iberia, La.	April, "		
12	73	Catholic Grave-yard, New Iberia, La.	April, "		
		Carried forward		124	Monument Cemetery, Chalmette, near New Orleans, La.

From Louisiana to Louisiana—Continued.

No.	Number of Graves.	NUMBER AND ORIGINAL LOCATION OF GRAVES. Original Location.	DATE OF REMOVAL OF BODIES.	FINAL DISPOSITION OF REMAINS. Number of Bodies.	Final Resting-Place.
		Brought forward...		124	
13	3	Episcopal Church-yard, ¼ mile west of New Iberia, La..	April, 1868		
14	1	Leon Frilow's plantation, 5¼ miles south of New Iberia, La...	April, "		
15	20	Mrs. Hopkin's place, New Iberia, La.............	April, "		
16	3	Mrs. Lewis' plantation, ¼ mile below New Iberia, La...	April, "		
17	5	Mr. Nelson's plantation, 3 miles southeast of New Iberia, La.	April, "		
18	1	D. Oliver's plantation, 3 miles south of New Iberia, La...	April, "		
19	1	Chas. Oliver's plantation, 3½ miles south of New Iberia, La..	April, "		
20	12	Mrs. Week's place, ¼ mile below New Iberia, La............	April, "		
21	1	P. C. Bethell's plantation, 5 miles north of Pattersonville, La..	April, "		
22	1	Mr. Cornay's plantation, 4 miles north of Pattersonville, La.	April, "		
23	25	Mrs. Knight's plantation, 3½ miles north of Pattersonville, La.	March, "		
24	1	Madam Meade's plantation, 3 miles north of Pattersonville, La.	April, "		
25	1	Mrs. Meade's upper plantation, 6 miles north of Pattersonville, La.	April, "		
26	1	Sarah Robin's plantation, ¼ mile north of Pattersonville, La...	April, "		
27	3	Maj. Weigbtman's plantation, left bank of Bayou Teche, 4½ miles north of Pattersonville, La.	April, "		
28	1	Orphans' Home Association, 4 miles north of Franklin, La..	April, "		
29	2	Perry Moses' plantation, 2 miles south of Vermillionville, La...	May, "		
30	3	L. Riggs' plantation, Vermillionville, La....................	May, "		
31	2	Madam Whitington's plantation, 2 miles south of Vermillionville, La.	May, "	127	Monument Cemetery, Chalmette, near New Orleans, La.
32	1	Capt. Little's plantation, 3 miles northwest of Barry's landing, parish of St. Landry, La...........			
33	6	Catholic burial-ground, Washington, parish of St. Landry, La..			
34	4	Methodist grave-yard, Opelousas, parish of St. Landry, La....			
35	4	R. Disretel's plantation, ¼ mile west of Barry's landing, parish of St. Landry, La............			
36	2	Prescott's plantation, near Washington, parish of St. Landry, La..			
37	3	Madam Dejean's plantation, ¼ mile east of Barry's landing, parish of St. Landry, La...			

15

38	1	Frezer's plantation, near Opelousas, parish of St. Landry, La.	} Month of June, 1868.		
39	1	J. P. Richard's plantation, near Opelousas, parish of St. Landry, La.			
40	1	Mr. Gidney's garden, Opelousas, parish of St. Landry, La.			
41	1	St. Clair's plantation, parish of St. Landry, La.			
42	2	Richard's plantation, near Opelousas, parish of St. Landry, La.			
43	1	Predon's plantation, near Opelousas, parish of St. Landry, La.			
44	1	Little's plantation, 2¾ miles west of Burry's landing, parish of St. Landry, La.			
45	2	J. Woodruff's plantation, near Grand Coteau, parish of St. Landry, La.			
46	2	Catholic burial-ground, town of Houma, Terrebonne parish, La.			
47	8	F. G. Fere's plantation, 4¼ miles west of Boutte Station, Opelousas railroad, St. Charles parish, La.			
		Total removed to Chalmette		251	

v.—From Texas to Texas.

1	42	Near Victoria, Tex.	April 8, 1868.		} Galveston National Cemetery, Tex.
2	50	Camp Sterling and Placido river, Tex.	April 23, "	118	
3	26	U. S. Cemetery, Lavaca, Tex.	April 30, "		
		Total removed to Galveston		118	
1	1	Post Hospital, Brownsville, Tex.	} From June 20 to June 27, 1868.	2	} Brownsville National Cemetery, Tex.
2	1	Fort Brown, Brownsville, Tex.			
		Total removed to Brownsville		2	
1	65	San Antonio, Tex. (City Cemetery)	Dec., 1867		} San Antonio National Cemetery, Tex. (Baxter county.)
2	55	Moedina river, Tex.	Jan., 1868	76	
3	25	Austin, Tex.	April, "		
4	31	Salado creek, Tex.	Jan., "		
		Total removed to San Antonio		76	

VI.—From Tennessee, Kentucky, Mississippi, and Alabama, to Tennessee.

No.	Number of Graves.	Number and Original Location of Graves.	Date of Removal of Bodies.	Final Disposition of Remains.	
		Original Location.		Number of Bodies.	Final Resting-place.
1	1	Adams' Station, Tenn. (N. and N. W. R. R.)			
2	1	Battle Hill, Tenn. (13 miles from Nashville)			
3	1	Beard's Ferry, Tenn. (On Duck river)			
4	699	Bowling Green Cemetery, Ky.			
5	322	Bowling Green, Ky. (U. S. Burial-ground)			
6	10	Bucks' Lodge Station, Tenn. (L. and N. R. R.)			
7	10	Burns' Station and vicinity, Tenn. (N. and N. W. R. R.)			
8	100	Carthage Cemetery, Tenn.			
9	26	Carthage vicinity, Tenn.			
10	3	Near Carthage, Tenn. (Across the river, north)			
11	17	Mrs. Goodall's farm, near Carthage, Tenn.			
12	13	Castilian Springs, Tenn. (8 miles from Gallatin)			
13	1	Mrs. Bates' farm, near Castilian Springs, Tenn.			
14	9	Cave City, Ky. (South of L. and N. R. R.)			
15	1	L. P. Taylor's farm, 8 miles from Cave City, Ky.			
16	6	Centreville, Tenn.			
17	6	Col. Durdan's farm, on the Centreville and Franklin pike, Tenn.			
18	1	Mayberry's burial ground, 8 miles west of Centreville, Tenn.			
19	1	Wade's farm, 7 miles southwest of Centreville, Tenn.			
20	5	Charlotte Cemetery, Tenn.			
21	1	Harpeth river, 3 miles north of Charlotte pike, Tenn.			
22	1	Hines' farm, Charlotte pike, Tenn.			
23	1	Shote's farm, 3 miles north of Charlotte pike, Tenn.			
24	4	Cherry Mound, Tenn. (29 miles south of Nashville)			
25	4	Mrs. Dunnie's farm, foot of Chestnut ridge, Tenn.			
26	1	Near Concord Church, Tenn. (Nolensville pike)			
27	1	Cumberland Furnace, Tenn.			
28	2	Mrs. Boomford's cemetery, near Dixon Springs, Tenn.			
29	26	Edgefield, Tenn. (Cemetery on Mr. McGranock's farm)			
30	2	A. Payne's farm, Edgefield Junction, Tenn.			
31	6	Fountain Head Church, Tenn. (L. and N. R. R.)			

17

No.		Location	Date	Remains	Cemetery
32	5	Franklin Cemetery, Ky			
33	1	Franklin pike, 4 miles north of Franklin, Ky			
34	1	Widow Larwe's farm, 2 miles southeast of Franklin, Ky			
35	2	Wood's farm, 2 miles southeast of Franklin, Ky			
36	745	Gallatin Cemetery, Tenn			
37	5	14 miles east of Gallatin, Tenn. (Hartsville pike)			
38	1	Christian Church, 5 miles from Gallatin, Tenn			
39	1	Johnson's farm, 5 miles from Gallatin, Tenn			
40	2	Rob's farm, 5 miles west of Gallatin, Tenn			
41	79	J. Sheppard's farm, 4 miles northeast of Gallatin, Tenn			
42	15	Gillem's Station, Tenn. (N. and N. W. R. R.)			
43	1	Mrs. Williams' farm, 3 miles north of Gillem's Station, Tenn			
44	1	Glendale Station, Tenn. (Catholic Cemetery)			
45	3	Cheatham's Mill, Green River Station, Tenn	Oct., 1867, to Jan., 1868.	7,006	Nashville National Cemetery, Tenn. (Davidson county.)
46	1	Hall's Mill Stockade, Tenn. (Bank of Mill creek)			
47	43	Hartsville Cemetery, Tenn			
48	1	Mrs. Beasley's farm, 6 miles east of Hartsville, Tenn			
49	1	McDaniel's farm, 3 miles from Hartsville, Tenn			
50	1	Gen'l Donelson's farm, near Henderson, Tenn			
51	9	Hutton's Chapel, Tenn			
52	1	Johnsonville, Tenn. (Near Wagoner's house)			
53	4	Near Johnsonville, Tenn. (Cemetery on hill)			
54	2	Near Johnsonville, Tenn. (On hill, near Government corrall)			
55	101	Near Johnsonville, Tenn. (U. S. Burial-ground)			
56	16	Near Johnsonville, Tenn. (On a ridge, between two forts)			
57	3	Opposite Rockford Ledge, 10 miles above Johnsonville, Tenn			
58	19	J. Winford's farm, near Johnsonville, Tenn			
59	19	Kingston Springs, Tenn. (N. and N. W. R. R.)			
60	30	McEwen's Station, Tenn. (Near Yellow Bank Trussel)			
61	26	Near McGowan's Station, Tenn. (N. and N. W. R. R.)			
62	30	Mitchelville vicinity, Tenn			
63	3,021	Nashville, Tenn. (City Cemetery)			
64	1,524	Nashville, Tenn. (Small-pox Cemetery)			
65	19	Nashville vicinity, Tenn			
66	1	Near Nashville, Tenn. (On Charlotte pike)			
67	1	Mrs. Allen's farm, 9 miles from Nashville, Tenn			
68	3	Mat. Anderson's farm, near Nashville, Tenn			
69	2	Berry's farm, 4 miles from Nashville, Tenn			
70	1	W. W. Berry's farm, 8 miles from Nashville, Tenn			
71	1	Blankall's farm, 3 miles from Nashville, Tenn			
		Carried forward		7,006	

Tennessee, Kentucky, Mississippi, and Alabama, to Tennessee—Continued.

No.	NUMBER AND ORIGINAL LOCATION OF GRAVES.		DATE OF REMOVAL OF BODIES.	FINAL DISPOSITION OF REMAINS.	
	Number of Graves.	Original Location.		Number of Bodies.	Final Resting-place.
		Brought forward............	....	7,006	
72	1	Boeley's farm, 4 miles from Nashville, Tenn..........			
73	1	Buford's farm, south of Nashville, Tenn..........			
74	1	J. Cartwright's farm, 10 miles from Nashville, Tenn..........			
75	1	Childer's farm, 3 miles from Nashville, Tenn..........			
76	1	Sam'l Davis' farm, 16 miles from Nashville, Tenn..........			
77	2	Mrs. Dobson's farm, 14 miles from Nashville, Tenn..........			
78	1	Ellis' farm, 9 miles from Nashville, Tenn..........			
79	1	Girdley's farm, 9 miles from Nashville, Tenn..........			
80	4	Greer's farm, 17 miles from Nashville, Tenn..........			
81	1	Capt. Hadley's farm, 11 miles from Nashville, Tenn..........			
82	2	Dr. Hawkit's farm, 10 miles from Nashville, Tenn..........			
83	1	Col. Hill's farm, 13 miles from Nashville, Tenn..........			
84	1	Holt's farm, 14 miles from Nashville, Tenn..........			
85	1	John House's farm, 16 miles from Nashville, Tenn..........			
86	2	Judge Humphrey's farm, 2 miles from Nashville, Tenn..........			
87	1	Mrs. Johnson's farm, 4 miles from Nashville, Tenn..........			
88	1	Jones' farm, 17 miles from Nashville, Tenn..........			
89	1	Lindsley's farm, bank of Cumberland, in view of Nashville, Tenn.			
90	1	Martin's farm, 5 miles from Nashville, Tenn..........			
91	1	McDaniel's farm, 11 miles from Nashville, Tenn..........			
92	1	McEwen's farm, 4 miles from Nashville, Tenn..........			
93	1	Mill creek, 7 miles from Nashville, Tenn..........			
94	2	Widow Moore's farm, 10 miles from Nashville, Tenn..........			
95	1	J. C. Owen's farm, 11 miles from Nashville, Tenn..........			
96	2	Squire Page's farm, 9 miles from Nashville, Tenn..........			
97	2	John Provine's farm, near Nashville, Tenn..........			
98	2	Rain's grave-yard, Tenn. (Nashville and Chattanooga R. R.)			
99	1	Ray's farm, 2 miles from Nashville, Tenn..........			
100	1	J. Reed's farm, 10 miles from Nashville, Tenn..........			
101	2	Stewart's Ferry pike, 8 miles from Nashville, Tenn..........			
102	1	Thompson's farm, 4 miles from Nashville, Tenn..........			

103	8,593	U. S. Burial-grounds, near Nashville, Tenn.	
104	1	Granny White pike, 10 miles from Nashville, Tenn.	
105	2	Nolensville Cemetery, Tenn.	
106	3	Pike House ferry, Tenn. (On Cumberland river)	
107	2	Red River bridge, Tenn. (In Stockade)	
108	3	Richland Station, Tenn. (L. and N. R. R.)	
109	1	Near Rock Hill Station, Ky. (L. and N. R. R.)	
110	39	T. Allen's farm, 7 miles from Rock Hill Station, Ky	
111	21	Scottsville, Ky. (U. S. Burial-ground)	
112	4	Smeedsville, Tenn. (100 yards east of depot)	
113	7	Smeedsville vicinity, Tenn. (North side of N. and N. W. R. R.)	
114	13	Smith's Grove, Ky. (L. and N. R. R.)	
115	4	South Tunnel, Tenn. (Catholic Burial-ground)	Oct., 1867, to Jan., 1868. 8,926
116	6	Springfield, Tenn. (Cemetery north of Court-house)	
117	3	Near Springfield, Tenn. (On Nashville pike)	
118	1	Mrs. Bank's farm, 2 miles south of Springfield, Tenn.	
119	5	John Camron's farm, near Springfield, Tenn.	
120	1	Capt. Heury's farm, 7 miles from Springfield, Tenn.	
121	1	Mrs. Irzer's farm, near Springfield, Tenn.	
122	34	Judge Lee's farm, near Springfield, Tenn.	
123	1	U. S. Burial-ground, near Springfield, Tenn.	
124	1	L. W. Willis' farm, 7 miles northeast of Springfield, Tenn.	
125	70	State Line Station, Tenn. (N. and N. W. R. R.)	
126	1	Triune vicinity, Tenn.	
127	1	Triune, Tenn.	
128	2	Copeland's farm, near Triune, Tenn.	
129	1	Perkins' farm, near Triune, Tenn.	
130	1	Dr. Scales' farm, 9 miles from Triune, Tenn.	
131	7	Signal Hill, near Triune, Tenn.	
132	4	Tyrn Springs, Tenn.	
133	15	W. Roberts' farm, near Tyrn Springs, Tenn	
134	25	Near Vernon, Tenn.	
135	1	Waverly and vicinity, Tenn.	
136	4	John Holland's farm, 4 miles from Waverly, Tenn.	
137	2	Trace creek, 3 miles from Waverly, Tenn.	
138	1	White's Bluff, Tenn. (N. and N. W. R. R.)	
139	1	J. Holman's farm, 4 miles from Woodbury, Ky	
140	1	R. D. Nicholas' farm, 3 miles south of Woodbury, Ky	
141	1	Woodland Church, near Woodbury, Ky	
		Total removed to Nashville Nashville National Cemetery, Tenn. (Davidson county.)	15,932

Tennessee, Kentucky, Mississippi, and Alabama, to Tennessee—Continued.

No.	Number of Graves.	NUMBER AND ORIGINAL LOCATION OF GRAVES. Original Location.	DATE OF REMOVAL OF BODIES.	FINAL DISPOSITION OF REMAINS.	
				Number of Bodies.	Final Resting-place.
1	1	Adamsville, Tenn. (In Burial-ground)			
2	1	Adamsville vicinity, Tenn			
3	1	Cedar Creek Landing, Tenn			
4	2	J. Clem's place, Cerro Gordo, Tenn			
5	4	Chickasaw, Miss			
6	1	Chickasaw, Miss. (Citizens' Grave-yard)			
7	1	Clifton, Tenn			
8	19	Clifton, Tenn. (In Burial-ground)			
9	5	Johnson's place, Clifton, Tenn			
10	12	On Corinth road, Tenn			
11	1	Craven's Landing, Tenn			
12	1	Craven's Landing, Tenn. (In Burial-ground)			
13	50	Crump's Landing, Tenn			
14	105	Eastport, Miss. (Hospital Burial-ground)			
15	26	Eastport, Tenn. (Scattered burials)			
16	6	Widow Emerson's place, opposite Eastport, Tenn			
17	5	Mr. Hill's place, near Eastport, Tenn			
18	13	Wheelock's place, near Eastport, Tenn			
19	1	Whitsell's place, near Eastport, Tenn			
20	30	Fort Heiman, Ky			
21	44	Fort Henry, Tenn			
22	8	Gravelly Springs, Tenn. (Hospital burials)			
23	25	Mr. Carroll's place, Gravelly Springs, Tenn			
24	2	Chandler's place, Gravelly Springs, Tenn			
25	6	Mr. Huston's place, Gravelly Springs, Tenn			
26	2	Mr. Proctor's place, Gravelly Springs, Tenn			
27	143	Hamburg, Tenn. (Hospital burials)			
28	5	Hamburg, vicinity, Tenn			
29	3	On Hamburg and Farmington road, Tenn			
30	3	Henry Barlow's place, Hamburg and Savannah road, Tenn			
31	1	Barnett's place, Hamburg and Farmington road, Tenn			

32	1	Moore's place, Hamburg and Farmington road, Tenn.	
33	1	Luther's place, Hamburg and Farmington road, Tenn.	
34	5	Springer's place, Hamburg and Farmington road, Tenn.	
35	1	Wm. Wood's place, Hamburg and Pen Ridge road, Tenn.	
36	184	Monterey City Cemetery, Tenn.	
37	5	Monterey vicinity, Tenn.	
38	6	Paris Landing, Tenn.	
39	2	Perryville, Tenn.	
40	455	Pittsburg Landing, Tenn. (Hospital Burial-ground.)	
41	3	Pittsburg Landing, Tenn. (Scattered burials.)	
42	1	J. Bentley's place, Pittsburg Landing, Tenn.	
43	25	Chamber's place, Pittsburg Landing and Corinth road, Tenn.	
44	21	D. S. Michie's place, near Pittsburg Landing, Tenn.	
45	9	R. W. Michie's place, near Pittsburg Landing, Tenn.	
46	104	Talliferro place, Pittsburg and Corinth road, Tenn.	
47	14	Mr. Walker's place, opposite Pittsburg Landing, Tenn.	
48	1	Saltillo, Tenn. (Citizens' Grave-yard.)	
49	310	Savannah, Tenn. (Hospital burials.)	
50	8	Bank of the river, near Savannah, Tenn.	
51	5	Boyle's place, near Savannah, Tenn.	
52	4	Boyle's Mill, near Savannah, Tenn.	
53	2	Cherry's place, near Savannah, Tenn.	
54	1	Dorin's place, near Savannah, Tenn.	
55	3	Hamilton's place, near Savannah, Tenn.	
56	8	Irvin's place, near Savannah, Tenn.	
57	1	Masonic Hall, Savannah, Tenn.	
58	15	Judge Walker's place, near Savannah, Tenn.	
59	564	Shiloh Battle-field, Tenn.	Shiloh National Cemetery, at Pittsburg Landing, Tenn. (Hardin county.) From Dec. 1, 1866, to April 1, 1868. 2,669
60	2	Shiloh Church, Tenn.	
61	34	Grave-yard at Shiloh Church, Tenn.	
62	35	Shiloh Church vicinity, Tenn.	
63	18	Mr. Barnes' place, Shiloh, Tenn.	
64	123	Widow Bell's place, Shiloh, Tenn.	
65	92	Larkin Bell's place, Shiloh, Tenn.	
66	6	J. Bell's place, Shiloh, Tenn.	
67	7	Jas. Bentley's place, Shiloh, Tenn.	
68	52	Mr. Blevin's place, Shiloh, Tenn.	
69	2	D. Brotherton's place, near Shiloh, Tenn.	
70	2	Brown's Ferry, Shiloh, Tenn.	
71	10	Mr. Contrell's place, Shiloh, Tenn.	
		Carried forward	2,669

Tennessee, Kentucky, Mississippi, and Alabama, to Tennessee—Continued.

No.	Number of Graves.	Number and Original Location of Graves. Original Location.	Date of Removal of Bodies.	Final Disposition of Remains. Number of Bodies.	Final Resting-place.
		Brought forward		2,669	
72	31	Cloud Farm, Shiloh, Tenn			
73	10	Dan'l Davis' place, Shiloh, Tenn			
74	9	Sarah Davis' place, Shiloh, Tenn			
75	40	Mr. Duncan's place, Shiloh, Tenn			
76	53	Wm. Edward's place, Shiloh, Tenn			
77	34	M. George's place, Shiloh, Tenn			
78	32	H. Hargrave's place, Shiloh, Tenn			
79	115	D. Harmon's place, Shiloh, Tenn			
80	22	D. Howell's place, Shiloh, Tenn			
81	2	Allen Jones' place, near Shiloh Church, Tenn			
82	115	Widow Jones' place, Shiloh, Tenn	From Dec. 1, 1866, to April 1, 1868.	875	Shiloh National Cemetery, at Pittsburg Landing, Tenn. (Hardin county.)
83	3	Henry Maxwell's place, Shiloh, Tenn			
84	2	Mr. McDonald's place, Shiloh, Tenn			
85	1	Stephen Moore's place, near Shiloh Church, Tenn			
86	91	Mr. Perry's place, Shiloh, Tenn			
87	1	D. Pickens' place, near Shiloh Church, Tenn			
88	16	Mr. Ray's place, Shiloh, Tenn			
89	7	Mr. Sea's place, near Shiloh Church, Tenn			
90	81	Geo. Sowell's place, Shiloh, Tenn			
91	20	W. Sowell's place, Shiloh, Tenn			
92	96	P. Spain's place, Shiloh, Tenn			
93	56	M. Spain's place, Shiloh, Tenn			
94	12	Mr. Traby's place, Shiloh, Tenn			
95	12	Widow Wicker's place, Shiloh, Tenn			
96	1	Swallow's Bluff, Miss			
97	4	Mr. Bundy's place, Wainesboro' road, Tenn			
98	8	Waterloo, Ala			
99	1	Mr. Higgin's place, Waterloo, Ala			
		Total removed to Shiloh		3,544	

23

No.	Count	Location	Date	Cemetery
1	1	Dover vicinity, Tenn. (Near Federal rifle pits)		
2	1	Dover vicinity, Tenn. (Winn's Ferry road)		
3	1	G. Einhard's garden, near Dover, Tenn		
4	1	Dover vicinity, Tenn. (Southeast of Randolph's forge and Dover road)		
5	1	Dover vicinity, Tenn. (North of Mr. Joslyn's house)		
6	1	Dover vicinity, Tenn. (South of Ridge road)		
7	3	Dover vicinity, Tenn. (Near Cooley's hotel)		
8	1	Dover vicinity, Tenn. (On north hill-side)		
9	133	Dover Grave-yard, Tenn		
10	8	3 miles from Dover, Tenn. (West of Mather's house)		
11	4	Dover vicinity, Tenn. (South of Mr. Walter's house)	No date given	Fort Donelson Nat'l Cemetery, Tenn.
12	27	Hospital at Rollin's house, 1¼ mile south of Dover, Tenn		
13	22	Robinson's Hill, Dover vicinity, Tenn		
14	5	Widow Cherry's land, 2 miles south of Dover, Tenn		
15	5	Dover vicinity, Tenn. (South bank of the Cumberland river)		
16	17	John Hinson's farm, 3 miles from Dover, Tenn		
17	2	Dover vicinity, Tenn. (South of Mr. Walter's house)		
18	285	Fort Donelson Battle-field, Tenn		
19	6	In Fort Donelson, Tenn		
20	62	Battle-field group, Fort Donelson, Tenn		
21	16	Widow Crisp's land, 2 miles west of Fort Donelson, Tenn		
22	10	West bank of the Cumberland, 3 miles below Fort Donelson, Tenn		
23	33	Hopkinsville, Ky. (City Cemetery)		
24	2	Joiner's family grave-yard, near La Fayette, Ky		
25	5	J. Wood's grave-yard, near Randolph's forge, Tenn		
	652	Total removed to Fort Donelson		652

VII.—From Kentucky to Kentucky.

No.	Count	Location	Date	Cemetery
1	38	Antioch Church, 8 miles from Perryville, Ky		
2	56	Camp Dick Robinson, Ky. (Near Robinson's house)	October and November, 1868.	Perryville National Cemetery, Ky. (Decatur county.)
3	1	Camp Dick Robinson, Ky. (Outside of Church Cemetery)		
4	3	Camp Dick Robinson, Ky. (Reform Church Cemetery)		
5	31	Harrodsburg, Ky. (Old Town Cemetery)		
6	2	Maxville Cemetery, Ky		
	331	Carried forward		331

From Kentucky to Kentucky—Continued.

No.	Number of Graves.	NUMBER AND ORIGINAL LOCATION OF GRAVES. Original Location.	DATE OF REMOVAL OF BODIES.	FINAL DISPOSITION OF REMAINS. Number of Bodies.	Final Resting-place.
		Brought forward		331	
7	40	Maxville road, Ky., (Near Perryville, on a side hill)			
8	1	Mrs. B. Hogg's place, Maxville, Ky			
9	1	Mrs. Niff's place, Nevada, Ky			
10	136	Perryville, Ky. (Hospital burial-ground, opposite Town Cemetery).			
11	1	Mrs. Allgood's house, near Perryville, Ky			
12	4	Wm. Beadle's land, near Perryville, Ky			
13	3	Sam'l Bottom's land, Perryville Battlefield, Ky			
14	192	H. P. Bottom's farm, Perryville Battle-field, Ky			
15	5	Green Bottom's land, near Perryville, Ky			
16	1	G. C. Bottom's land, near Perryville, Ky			
17	14	Mr. Broyle's farm, near Perryville, Ky			
18	42	Jacob Capenter's land, near Perryville, Ky. (Hospital burial-ground)			
19	38	Donelly's farm, near Perryville, Ky	October and November, 1868.	643	Perryville National Cemetery, Ky. (Decatur county.)
20	3	Widow Elder's family grave-yard, near Perryville, Ky			
21	3	Jerry Gibson's farm, near Perryville, Ky			
22	8	Peter Harmon's farm, near Perryville, Ky			
23	2	Elihu Jett's land, near Perryville, Ky			
24	1	Kingeray place, 12 miles from Perryville, Ky			
25	5	L. Martin's place, near Perryville, Ky			
26	6	McGraw's farm, Perryville Battle-field, Ky			
27	15	Jordan Peter's farm, near Perryville, Ky			
28	8	Chas. Powell's farm, near Perryville, Ky			
29	1	J. L. Powell's farm, near Perryville, Ky			
30	89	Russell's farm, Perryville Battle-field, Ky			
31	1	Rear of Sanderford's blacksmith shop, 7 miles from Perryville, Ky			
32	22	Seminary Hospital, near Perryville, Ky			
33	1	John Sutherland's farm, near Perryville, Ky			
34	20	Town Cemetery Hospital, near Perryville, Ky			

25

No.	Count	Location	Period	Total
35	33	Turpin's farm, near Perryville, Ky		
36	1	Ward's place, near Perryville, Ky		
37	1	E. White's land, near Perryville, Ky		
38	137	Wilkinson's farm, Perryville battlefield, Ky		
39	1	Mr. Williams' family grave-yard, near Perryville, Ky		
40	7	Springfield, Ky. (Town Cemetery)		
		Total removed to Perryville		974
1	2	Bacon creek, Ky. (Camp-ground, north of Church)		
2	2	Near Bacon Creek Station, Ky. (East of L. and N. R. R.)		
3	2	Near Bacon Creek Station, Ky. (In a ravine)		
4	3	W. R. Gibson's farm, near Bacon Creek Station, Ky		
5	5	Mrs. Houston's farm, near Bacon Creek Station, Ky		
6	7	Judge Jimison's farm, near Bacon Creek Station, Ky		
7	1	W. T. Wright's farm, near Bacon Creek Station, Ky		
8	1	Lewis Wright's farm, near Bacon Creek Station, Ky		
9	19	Near Belmont Furnace, Ky. (In citizen's grave-yard, 2 miles east of L. and N. R. R.)		
10	4	S. Pursell's family grave-yard, near Belmont Station, Ky	June and July, 1867.	3,700
11	3,172	Cave Hill Cemetery, Louisville, Ky		
12	1	Near Colesburg, Ky. (St. Clair Church-yard)		
13	1	Mrs. F. Amber's garden, 3 miles northeast of Colesburg, Ky		
14	19	Mr. J Crawford's farm, 4 miles northeast of Colesburg, Ky		
15	7	Fort Boyle, near Colesburg, Ky		
16	15	Fort Sands, near Colesburg, Ky		
17	26	Near Rolling Fork R. R. bridge, 3 miles northeast of Colesburg, Ky		
18	95	Elizabethtown Cemetery, Ky		
19	3	Henderson, Ky. (City Cemetery)		
20	4	Mount Moriah Church, 4 miles east of Lebanon Junction, Ky		
21	187	Wm. Orme's farm, 2 miles southwest of Lebanon Junction, Ky		
22	47	Mumfordsville, Ky. (Town Cemetery)		
23	13	Near Mumfordsville, Ky. (By Dr. Jett's house)		
24	5	Near Mumfordsville, Ky. (At a stone quarry west of town)		
25		Near Mumfordsville, Ky. (East of L. and N. R. R. crossing Green river)		
26	33	Dobson's farm, Mumfordsville, Ky		
27	21	Fort Willich, near Mumfordsville, Ky		
28	4	Col. Wood's farm, near Mumfordsville, Ky		
		Carried forward		3,700

Cave Hill National Cemetery, Louisville, Jefferson county, Ky.

From Kentucky to Kentucky—Continued.

No.	Number of Graves.	NUMBER AND ORIGINAL LOCATION OF GRAVES. Original Location.	DATE OF REMOVAL OF BODIES.	Number of Bodies.	FINAL DISPOSITION OF REMAINS. Final Resting-place.
		Brought forward.................................		3,700	
29	11	Nolin Station, Ky. (Gilead Church-yard)........			
30	1	Near Nolin Station, Ky. (In a woods, east of L. and N. R. R.)			
31	1	Near Nolin Station, Ky. (On a bluff, east of L. and N. R. R.)			
32	41	Owensboro', Ky. (Old town Cemetery street).......			
33	5	Owensboro', Ky. (Old Fair grounds)...............			
34	1	Owensboro', Ky. (New Cemetery).................			
35	43	Near Red Mills, Ky. (West of Citizens' grave-yard)			
36	1	Near Red Mills, Ky. (Up the creek, near McCraig's Mill)			
37	2	Near Red Mills, Ky. (L. and N. pike).............	June and July, 1867.	206	Cave Hill National Cemetery, Louisville, Jefferson county, Ky.
38	9	Mr. Lucas' farm, near Red Mills, Ky.............			
39	1	W. Williams' burying-ground, 3 miles northeast of Red Mills, Ky.			
40	5	Shepperdsville, Ky. (Town Cemetery)............			
41	8	Near Shepperdsville, Ky. (South side of Salt river, west of Railroad Station).			
42	1	Sonora, Ky. (Town grave-yard)...................			
43	3	J. T. Brawner's farm, near Sonora Station, Ky...			
44	4	Near Woodsonville, Ky. (At the Fort).............			
45	38	Near Woodsonville, Ky. (In an old Meeting-house Cemetery)			
46	21	A. L. Woodson's farm, Woodsonville, Ky.........			
		Total removed to Cave Hill.................		3,906	
1	1	Beaver Post, Ky. (14 miles southwest of Camp Burnside)			
2	42	Camp Burnside, Ky. (Post burial-ground).........			
3	26	Camp Burnside, Ky. (Colored burial-ground).....			
4	4	Camp Burnside, Ky. (Outside the Breastworks, near Mr. Early's.)			
5	6	Camp Burnside, Ky. (Near Cumberland river ferry)			
6	2	Camp Burnside, Ky. (East of S. H. Tait's house, on Jacksboro' road)			

7	13	Camp Green, Ky. (Mouth of Greasy creek, west bank of Cumberland river)	
8	140	Columbia, Ky. (Town Cemetery)	
9	1	Bear Wallow Meeting-house, 6 miles east of Columbia, Ky.	
10	1	Bethel Church grave-yard, 10 miles southeast of Columbia, Ky.	
11	60	College vicinity, near Columbia, Ky.	
12	1	Widow Connor's farm, 3¼ miles west of Columbia, Ky.	
13	1	B. Grant's family grave-yard, 4 miles north of Columbia, Ky.	
14	1	Holiday family grave-yard, 4 miles east of Columbia, Ky.	
15	2	Miller's family grave-yard, 10 miles south of Columbia, Ky.	
16	1	Mr. Russell's farm, near Columbia, Ky.	
17	1	Widow Stoll's family grave-yard, 4 miles from Columbia, Ky.	
18	7	Tabor church, 3¼ miles south of Columbia, Ky.	
19	1	North of Toll-gate, near Columbia, Ky.	
20	1	J. McWilliam's farm, 13 miles from Crab Orchard, Ky.	
21	3	Freedom Meeting-house, Ky. (6 miles south of Rowena road)	June, July, August, October, and Nov., '67.
22	5	J.W. Coffee's farm, Greasy Creek battlefield, Ky.	
23	1	J. Norfleet's grave-yard, near Harrison, Ky.	
24	1	Hereford River Bottom, Ky. (6 miles from Wolf creek)	
25	8	Jamestown, Ky. (Town Cemetery)	
26	1	J. Carter's grave-yard, 7 miles west of Jamestown, Ky.	
27	1	5 miles northeast of Logan's X Road's, Ky. (Near the mouth of Cold Weather creek)	
28	1	Collin's family grave-yard, Logan's X Road's, Ky.	
29	1	Fishing Creek Meeting-house, 5½ miles northeast of Logan's X Roads, Ky.	Mill Springs National Cemetery, Logan's X Roads, Wayne county, Ky.
30	1	Morrow family grave-yard, 18 miles southwest of Logan's X Roads, Ky.	
31	1	Stevens' family grave-yard, 10 miles from Logan's X Roads, Ky.	
32	1	Weddle's family grave-yard, Logan's X Roads, Ky.	
33	36	Mill Springs battlefield, Ky.	
34	2	Mill Springs Ferry, Ky. (Along the north bank of the Cumberland river)	
35	7	Opposite Mill Springs, Ky. (North bank of Cumberland river)	
36	7	Mr. West's family grave-yard, near Mill Springs, Ky.	
37	2	Monticello, Ky. (Town Cemetery)	
38	1	Newell's ferry, Ky. (On the Cumberland river, 2 miles from Waitsboro')	
39	1	Lindsey Sawyer's farm, ¼ mile northwest of Ringold School-house, Ky.	
		Carried forward	393

28

From Kentucky to Kentucky—Continued.

No.	Number of Graves.	Number and Original Location of Graves. Original Location.	Date of Removal of Bodies.	Number of Bodies.	Final Disposition of Remains. Final Resting-place.
		Brought forward		393	
40	2	Salem Meeting-house, Ky. (13 miles from Somerset)			
41	6	Near Shiloh Church, Ky. (2½ miles from old Glasgow road)			
42	208	Somerset, Ky. (Baptist Church grave-yard)			
43	1	Somerset, Ky. (New Cemetery)			
44	16	Near Somerset, Ky. (On the Common, in the vicinity of S. H. Porch's)			
45	1	Somerset vicinity, Ky. (East of Fishing creek, on road to Logan's X Roads)			
46	8	Capt. J. Bellows' farm, Somerset vicinity, Ky	June, July, August, October, and Nov., '67.	308	Mill Springs National Cemetery, Logan's X Roads, Wayne county, Ky.
47	1	Widow Bishop's grave-yard, near Somerset, Ky			
48	1	Cowan grave-yard, 2½ miles from Somerset, Ky. (Monticello road)			
49	1	W. Durham's farm, near Somerset, Ky			
50	1	Dutton's grave-yard, near Somerset, Ky			
51	1	Flat Lick Church-yard, 11 miles northeast of Somerset, Ky			
52	13	Girdley farm, Dutton Hill battlefield, near Somerset, Ky			
53	1	D. F. James' farm, 7 miles northeast of Somerset, Ky			
54	1	Wm. McClaunche's farm, 22 miles east of Somerset, Ky			
55	1	McQuerry's grave-yard, 8 miles northeast of Somerset, Ky			
56	1	Nunnelly's farm, east of Waitsboro' road, near Somerset, Ky			
57	9	Pisgah Church-yard, near Somerset, Ky			
58	1	Price family grave-yard, 7 miles from Somerset, Ky			
59	1	S. H. Renfro's farm, 12 miles east of Somerset, Ky			
60	1	S. Rexroot's grave-yard, 20 miles east of Somerset, Ky			
61	2	Ringold School-house, 3 miles west of Somerset, Ky			
62	1	Wm. Roy's grave-yard, 25 miles south of Somerset, Ky			
63	5	Wm. A. Sallie's farm, near Somerset, Ky			
64	2	Widow Smith's grave-yard, 7½ miles north of Somerset, Ky			
65	1	E. Stevens' grave-yard, 7 miles east of Somerset, Ky			
66	1	Union Meeting-house, 6 miles northeast of Somerset, Ky			

29

#	Count	Location	Date	Subtotal	Destination
67	1	Vaughts' grave-yard, 3½ miles west of Somerset, Ky			
68	1	Stigall's Ferry, Ky. (Ravine, near Waitsboro')			
69	16	Waitsboro' vicinity, Ky. (Bank of Cumberland river)			
70	1	T. M. Cooper's farm, 8 miles below Waitsboro', Ky			
71	1	Henry White's farm, Ky. (3¾ miles northwest of Stanford and Salt Works road)			
		Total removed to Mill Springs		701	
1	1	Canton, Ky. (Southeast of Station, K. C. R. R.)			
2	21	Cynthiana Cemetery, Ky			
3	1	Toll-gate, near Cynthiana, Ky			
4	6	Falmouth, Ky. (Near Station, K. C. R. R.)			
5	3	Falmouth, Ky. (Citizens' grave-yard)			
6	1	Falmouth, Ky. (Near the Stockade, south bank of the Licking)			
7	672	Lexington City Cemetery, Ky. (Original interments. Not removed)			
8	31	Major Shelby's farm, 11 miles east of Lexington, Ky	Sept. and Oct., 1867.	822	Lexington National Cemetery, Ky. (Fayette county.)
9	9	Mount Sterling, Ky. (Old Town Cemetery)			
10	1	Mount Sterling, Ky. (New Cemetery)			
11	2	Judge Apperson's farm, near Mount Sterling, Ky			
12	6	Mrs. V. Botts' farm, near Mount Sterling, Ky			
13	2	A. Chenault's farm, near Mount Sterling, Ky			
14	2	J. Cockrell's farm, near Mount Sterling, Ky			
15	2	Wm. Tipton's farm, near Mount Sterling, Ky			
16	3	Mrs. Tipton's farm, near Mount Sterling, Ky			
17	1	J. D. Wilson's farm, near Mount Sterling, Ky			
18	37	Paris Cemetery, Ky			
19	11	Mathew Howard's farm, near Paris, Ky			
20	4	Town Cemetery, near Winchester, Ky			
21	3	15 miles from Mount Sterling, Ky. (On a dirt road in the woods.)			
22	4	On a ridge, southwest side of K. C. R. R. track, between Shanhan Station and the railroad bridge, Ky			
		Total removed to Lexington		822	

VIII.—From Michigan to Michigan.

No.	Number and Original Location of Graves.		Date of Removal of Bodies.	Final Disposition of Remains.	
	Number of Graves.	Original Location.		Number of Bodies.	Final Resting-place.
1	2	Silver Creek Cemetery, Niles, Mich.	During April, 1868.	23	Fort Wayne National Cemetery, Mich.
2	8	New Cemetery at Kalamazoo, Mich.			
3	8	Old City Cemetery, Ypsilanti, Mich.			
4	5	Old Cemetery at Flint, Mich.			
		Total removed to Fort Wayne		23	

IX.—From Missouri and Arkansas to Missouri.

No.	Number of Graves.	Original Location.
1	265	Cape Girardeau, Mo. (City Cemetery)
2	2	J. Painter's farm, near Cape Girardeau, Mo.
3	2	2 miles south of Chalk Bluff, Ark. (In grave-yard)
4	1	S. Dallon's farm, near Chalk Bluff, Ark.
5	2	J. L. Moore's farm, near Charleston, Mo.
6	1	2¼ miles south of Cole Camp, Mo. (Benton county)
7	19	Columbia, Boone county, Mo. (City Cemetery)
8	1	J. S. Rollins' land, ¾ mile southeast of Columbia, Mo.
9	3	Dunklin county, Mo. (Near Chalk Bluff and Four-Mile road)
10	1	Fayette City Cemetery, Mo.
11	2	Freeland grave-yard, 2 miles northeast of Fayette, Mo.
12	1	5 miles northeast of Fulton, Mo.
13	5	7 miles northeast of Fulton, Mo. (Callaway county)
14	5	Cemetery ¼ mile east of Fulton, Mo.
15	2	J. Klenkler's land, 2 miles north of Pilot Grove, Mo. (Cooper county)
16	8	Wm. Parcell's lot, Kirksville, Adair county, Mo.
17	2	John Rolfa's land, Liberty township, Mo. (Cole county)
18	1	North bank of Osage river, 4 miles east of Lime creek, Mo.

19	1	South bank of Osage river, 2 miles east of Lime creek, Mo.	Mar. 24 to May 15, 1868.	379	Jefferson Barracks National Cemetery, St. Louis county, Mo.
20	1	Davis' grave-yard, 8 miles southeast of Lime creek, Mo.		
21	9	McClurg, Murphy, & Co's land, ¼ mile north of Lime creek, Mo.		
22	1	Mrs. Shepard's land, ¼ mile south of Lime creek, Mo.		
23	8	John Crawford's land, ¼ mile east of Rockport, Mo.		
24	1	Mr. Rollins' land, 2 miles southwest of Rockport, Mo.		
25	3	St. Genevieve Cemetery, Mo.		
26	1	H. Hirsch's land, 4 miles west of St. Genevieve, Mo.		
27	1	Mrs. J. McNeil's farm, 2 miles south of Scatterville, Ark.		
28	1	Near Miller's Mill, Stoddard county, Mo.		
29	9	Warsaw Cemetery, Mo.		
30	1	South bank of Osage river, opposite Warsaw, Mo.		
31	2	9 miles southwest of Warsaw, Mo.		
32	3	E. B. Cunningham's land, 8 miles south of Warsaw, Mo.		
33	6	Jenkins' grave-yard, 17 miles south of Warsaw, Mo.		
34	3	David Kidwell's land, 7 miles south of Warsaw, Mo.		
35	1	J. Opdycke's land, ¼ mile east of Warsaw, Mo.		
36	1	N. M. Steorit's land, 4 miles north of Warsaw, Mo.		
37	2	Wm. H. Stewart's land, 6 miles northeast of Warsaw, Mo.		
38	1	Wm. Wainwright's land, 15 miles south of Warsaw, Mo.		
		Total removed to Jefferson Barracks		379
1	1	Newton Alexander's land, 8 miles southeast of Bloomfield, Wright county, Mo.	From April 27 to June 9, '68.	35	Springfield National Cemetery, Greene county, Mo.
2	1	J. C. Trimble's land, 1¼ mile west of Bloomfield, Mo.		
3	2	Williams' grave-yard, 10 miles south of Bloomfield, Mo.		
4	3	A. J. Cochran's farm, near Coon creek, Barton county, Mo.		
5	3	Carthage, Jasper county, Mo.		
6	5	Carthage, Mo. (Public Cemetery)		
7	3	Tibang's farm, ¼ mile east of Elk Mills, McDonald county, Mo.		
8	3	South of Tilbang's farm, near Elk Mills, Mo. (In brush, 75 yards west of road)		
9	7	John Langley's farm, 2 miles north of Enterprise, McDonald county, Mo.		
10	2	Wm. Langley's farm, 3 miles north of Enterprise, Mo.		
11	2	Forsythe grave-yard, Christian county, Mo.		
12	2	Wm. Adams' farm, 10 miles northeast of Forsythe, Mo.		
13	1	Thos. Casey's land, 2 miles east of Forsythe, Mo.		
		Carried forward		35

From Missouri and Arkansas to Missouri—Continued.

No.	Number of Graves.	NUMBER AND ORIGINAL LOCATION OF GRAVES. Original Location.	DATE OF REMOVAL OF BODIES.	FINAL DISPOSITION OF REMAINS. Number of Bodies.	Final Resting-place.
		Brought forward		35	
14	2	D. D. Clements' farm, 10 miles north of Forsythe, Mo. (In Taney county)			
15	1	Widow Gunlin's land, 18 miles east of Forsythe, Mo. (In Douglas county)			
16	2	J. M. Hilton's land, 8¼ miles northwest of Forsythe, Mo.			
17	1	Fernando Moore's land, 9 miles northwest of Forsythe, Mo.			
18	16	B. P. Parish's land, Forsythe, Mo.			
19	1	G. W. Thurmar's land, south bank of White river, 2 miles east of Forsythe, Mo.			
20	17	J. Warmack's land, north bank of White river, Forsythe, Mo.			
21	1	Squire Willard's land, 13 miles northeast of Forsythe, Mo.			
22	2	A. Wilson's land, 1¼ mile south of Forsythe, Mo.			
23	7	Shirley's Ford battlefield, near Georgia City, Jasper county, Mo.			
24	6	Greenfield Town Cemetery, Dale county, Mo.			
25	1	C. M. Bradshaw's land, 15 miles west of Hartsville, Webster county, Mo.			
26	12	C. C. Goomar's land, Hartsville, Mo.			
27	2	Simeon Phillips' land, 20 miles southeast of Hartsville, Wright county, Mo.			
28	1	Joseph Reney's land, 3 miles northeast of Hartsville, Mo.			
29	1	Speculator's land, 10 miles south of Hartsville, Mo.			
30	3	Jasper county, Mo. (South bank of Dry Fork of Spring river)			
31	3	Lamar, Barton county, Mo. (400 yards west of Court-house)			
32	1	Lamar, Mo. (1½ mile south of Court-house)			
33	1	John Winkle's farm, 4 miles north of Lamar, Mo.			
34	1	Hoosier Prairie, Lawrence county, Mo.			
35	1	McDonald county, Mo. (In brush, ¼ mile south of Langley place, and 200 yards west of Cow Skin river)			
36	1	Marionsville, Mo. (Public Cemetery)			
37	2	Buck Prairie Church-yard, 2 miles southeast of Marionsville, Mo.			

33

38	7	Marshfield grave-yard, Webster county, Mo.		
39	2	Near Minersville, Jasper county, Mo.		
40	4	Mount Vernon, Mo. (Public Cemetery)		
41	3	Durnell's farm, Mount Vernon, Mo.		
42	6	Tallifero's farm, 7 miles north of Mount Vernon, Mo.		
43	77	Craig's farm, ¾ mile north of Neosho, Mo.		
44	2	Gibson's burial-ground, 1¼ mile northwest of Neosho, Mo.		
45	2	Herald's farm, ¼ mile east of Neosho, Mo.		
46	1	South bank Hickory creek, ¼ mile north of Neosho, Mo.		
47	1	Poole's Prairie, 4 miles east of Neosho, Mo.		
48	2	Capt. Ruark's barn-yard, near Neosho, Mo.		
49	24	Newtonia, Newton county, Mo. (Public Cemetery)		
50	1	Este's farm, 9 miles south of Newtonia, Mo.	From April 27 to June 9, '68.	268	Springfield National Cemetery, Greene county, Mo.
51	2	Fowler's farm, 2 miles southeast of Newtonia, Mo.		
52	1	Oliver's Prairie, near Newtonia, Mo. (1 mile south of Judge Ritchie's saw mill)		
53	1	M. Ritchie's field, near Newtonia, Mo. (¼ mile south of Neosho road)		
54	1	Cemetery near Oregon, Mo.		
55	1	Spring River Bottom, near Oregon, Mo.		
56	8	Ozark grave-yard, Christian county, Mo.		
57	1	Widow Cox's farm, south of Ozark, Mo.		
58	1	Pineville, McDonald county, Mo. (Cemetery west of Courthouse)		
59	2	Near Pineville, Mo. (2 miles west of Mr. Bell's house)		
60	1	Near Pineville, Mo. (¾ mile west of Mr. Seeboon's house)		
61	1	Preston, Jasper county, Mo. (On prairie, 1 mile north of town)		
62	11	In woods, ¼ mile west of Sarcoxie, Mo.		
63	2	Public Cemetery, ¾ mile southeast of Sarcoxie, Mo.		
64	1	Nancy Brott's land, 10 miles southwest of Springfield, Mo.		
65	1	Calvin Howard's land, 12 miles southwest of Springfield, Mo.		
66	3	Newbill place, 3 miles west of Springfield, Mo.		
67	1	Railroad land, 13 miles northeast of Springfield, Mo.		
68	1	P. Whitlock's land, 12 miles northeast of Springfield, Mo.		
69	5	Vera Cruz, Mo. (North side of, and on land belonging to town)		
70	1	5 miles east of Vera Cruz, Mo. (On Government land)		
71	2	Widow Lyon's land, 18 miles southwest of Vera Cruz, Mo. (In Douglas county)		
72	2	W. S. Babcock's land, 5 miles south of Vera Cruz, Mo.		
		Carried forward		303

From Missouri and Arkansas to Missouri—Continued.

No.	Number and Original Location of Graves.		Date of Removal of Bodies.	Final Disposition of Remains.	
	Number of Graves.	Original Location.		Number of Bodies.	Final Resting-place.
		Brought forward............		303	
73	1	Newton Turley's land, 7 miles north of Vera Cruz, Mo.	From April 27 to June 9, '68.	7	Springfield National Cemetery, Greene county, Mo.
74	2	Verona grave-yard, Mo. (South of School-house)...			
75	4	Near Verona, Mo. (300 yards south of Spring river)...			
		Total removed to Springfield............		310	

X.—From Montana Territory to Montana Territory.

No.	Number of Graves.	Original Location.	Date of Removal of Bodies.	Number of Bodies.	Final Resting-place.
1	5	Immediately adjacent to Fort Shaw, Montana Territory...	186—	5	Fort Shaw, Montana Territory.
		Total removed to Fort Shaw............		5	

ALPHABETICAL INDEX

TO

ORIGINAL PLACES OF BURIAL, WHENCE BODIES HAVE BEEN REMOVED.

Name of Locality.	Page.	Name of Locality.	Page.
Acworth, Ga.	9	Catesville, Ga.	11
Adair county, Mo.	20	Cave City, Ky.	16
Adam's Station, Tenn.	16	Cave Hill, Ky.	25
Adamsville, Tenn.	20	Cedar Creek Landing, Tenn.	20
Alexander, Ga.	11	Cedartown, Ga.	9
Allatoona, Ga.	9	Centreville, Tenn.	16
Antioch Church, Tenn.	23	Cerro Gordo, Tenn.	20
Augusta, Ga.	10	Chalk Bluff, Ark.	30
Athens, Ga.	9	Charleston, Mo.	30
Atlanta, Ga.	9	Charlotte, Tenn.	16
Austin, Tex.	15	Charlotte, N. C.	8
		Chatooga, Ala.	10
Bacon creek, Ky.	25	Cheatham's Mill, Tenn.	17
Barton county, Mo.	32	Cherokee county, Ala.	10
Bartow, Ga.	8	Cherry Mound, Tenn.	16
Battle Hill, Tenn.	16	Chestnut Ridge, Tenn.	16
Bayou Teche, La.	13–14	Chickasaw, Miss.	20
Bear Creek Station, Ga.	10	Christian county, Mo.	31–33
Beard's Ferry, Tenn.	16	Clarksville, Ark.	12
Bear Wallow, Ky.	27	Clifton, Tenn.	20
Beaver Post, Ky.	26	Cloutierville, La.	13
Belmont Furnace, Ky.	25	Cole Camp, Mo.	30
Belmont Station, Ky.	25	Colesburg, Ky.	25
Benton county, Mo.	30	Columbia, Ky.	27
Berwick, La.	13	Columbia, Mo.	30
Bethel, Ky.	27	Concord, Tenn.	16
Big Buckhead Bridge, Ga.	11	Coon creek, Mo.	31
Big Shanty, Ga.	9	Cooper county, Mo.	30
Black Jack Ridge, Ark.	12	Coosa river, Ga.	9
Bloomfield, Mo.	31	Corinth road, Tenn.	20
Bowling Green, Tenn.	16	Cotile Landing, La.	13
Brownsville, Tex.	15	Crab Orchard, Ky.	27
Buck's Lodge Station, Tenn.	16	Craven's Landing, Tenn.	20
Buck Prairie, Mo.	32	Crump's Landing, Tenn.	20
Burns' Station, Tenn.	16	Cumberland Furnace, Tenn.	16
		Cynthiana, Ky.	29
Calhoun, Ga.	9		
Callaway county, Mo.	30	Dahlonego, Tenn.	10
Campbell county, Ga.	10	Dale county, Mo.	32
Camp Burnside, Ky.	26	Dallas, Ga.	9
Camp Dick Robinson, Tenn.	23	Davidsboro', Ga.	8
Camp Green, Ky.	27	Decatur, Ga.	10
Camp Sterling, Tex.	15	De Kalb county, Ala.	10
Camp York, N. C.	8	Dixon Springs, Tenn.	16
Canton, Ky.	29	Douglas county, Mo.	32–33
Cape Girardeau, Mo.	30	Dover, Tenn.	23
Carthage, Tenn.	16	Dunklin county, Mo.	30
Carthage, Mo.	31	Dutches creek, Ark.	12
Carroll county, Ga.	10	Dutton Hill, Ky.	28
Carrollton, Ga.	10		
Cartersville, Ga.	9	East Point, Ga.	10
Castilian Springs, Tenn.	16	Eastport, Miss.	20

Name of Locality.	Page.	Name of Locality.	Page.
Edgefield, Tenn	16	Judson, Ala	10
Elizabethtown, Ky	25		
Elk Mills, Mo	31	Kalamazoo, Mich	30
Enterprise, Mo	31	Kenesaw, Ga	9
Eutoy creek, Ga	9	Kingston Springs, Tenn	17
Ezra Church, Ga	9	Kirksville, Mo	30
Falmouth, Ky	29	La Fayette, Ky	23
Fayette, Mo	30	Lamar, Mo	32
Fayette county, Ga	10	Lavaca, Tex	15
Fishing creek, Ky	27	Lawrence county, Mo	32
Flint, Mich	30	Lawton, Ga	11
Floyd county, Ga	10	Lebanon, Ala	10
Forsythe, Mo	31–32	Lebanon Junction, Ky	25
Fort Boyle, Ky	25	Lexington, N. C	8
Fort Donelson, Tenn	23	Lexington, Ky	29
Fort Heiman, Ky	20	Liberty Township, Mo	30
Fort Henry, Tenn	20	Lime creek, Mo	30
Fort Sands, Ky	25	Logan's X Roads, Ky	27
Fort Shaw, Montana	34	Lost Mountain, Ga	10
Fort Willach, Ky	25	Louisville, Ky	25
Fountain Head, Tenn	16	Lovejoy Station, Ga	10
Franklin, La	13–14		
Franklin, Ga	10	McDonald county, Mo	32–33
Franklin, Ky	17	McEwen's Station, Tenn	17
Freedom, Ky	27	McGowan's Station, Tenn	17
Freeland, Mo	30	Marietta, Ga	9
Fulton, Mo	30	Mansfield, La	13
		Marionsville, Mo	32
Gainesville, Ga	10	Marshfield, Mo	33
Gallatin, Tenn	17	Maxville, Tenn	23–24
Georgia City, Mo	32	Merryfield, Ga	11
Gillem's Station, Tenn	17	Mill creek, Tenn	18
Glendale Station, Tenn	17	Millen, Ga	11
Gold Hill, N. C	8	Mill Springs, Ky	27
Grand Coteau, La	13–15	Minersville, Mo	33
Grand Ecore, La	13	Mitchelville, Tenn	17
Gravelly Springs, Tenn	20	Moedina river, Tex	15
Greasy creek, Ky	27	Monterey, Tenn	21
Greenfield, Mo	32	Monticello, Ky	27
Green River Station, Tenn	17	Mott's Ferry, La	13
		Mount Moriah, Ky	25
Hack's Mills, Ga	11	Mount Sterling, Ky	29
Hall's Mill, Tenn	17	Mount Vernon, Mo	33
Hamburg, Tenn	20–21	Munfordsville, Ky	25
Harelson county, Ga	10		
Harpeth river, Tenn	16	Nashville, Tenn	17–18–19
Harrodsburg, Tenn	23	Natchitoches, La	13
Harrison, Ky	27	Neosho, Mo	33
Hartsville, Mo	32	Nevada, Tenn	24
Hartsville, Tenn	17	Newell's Ferry, Ky	27
Hawkinsville, Ga	8	New Hope Church, Ga	9
Henderson, Ky	25	New Iberia, La	13–14
Henderson, Tenn	17	Newnan, Ga	10
Hereforde River Bottom, Ky	27	Newton county, Mo	33
Hoosier Prairie, Mo	32	Newtonia, Mo	33
Hopkinsville, Ky	23	Niles, Mich	30
Horse Head creek, Ark	12	Nolensville, Tenn	19
Hutton's Chapel, Tenn	17	Nolin Station, Ky	26
Jamestown, Ky	27	Oliver's Prairie, Mo	33
Jasper county, Mo	32	Opelousas, La	15
Johnsonville, Tenn	17	Oregon, Mo	33
Jonesboro', Ga	9	Owensboro', Ky	26

Name of Locality.	Page.	Name of Locality.	Page.
Ozark, Mo	33	Silver creek, Ark	12
		Smeedsville, Tenn	19
Paris, Ky	29	Smith, Ark	12
Paris Landing, Tenn	21	Smith's Grove, Ky	19
Pattersonville, La	14	Somerset, Ky	28
Peachtree creek, Ga	9	Sonora, Ky	26
Perryville, Tenn	21-23-24-25	South Tunnel, Tenn	19
Pike House Ferry, Tenn	19	Springfield, Mo	33
Pilot Grove, Mo	30	Springfield, Ky	25
Pine Mountain, Ga	9	Springfield, Tenn	19
Pineville, Mo	33	State Line Station, Tenn	19
Pisgah Church, Ky	28	Station No. 7, C. R. R., Ga	11
Pittsburg Landing, Tenn	21	Station No. 9, C. R. R., Ga	11
Placido river, Tex	15	Station No. 9½, C. R. R., Ga	8
Pleasant Hill, La	13	Stigall's Ferry, Ky	29
Polk county, Ga	9	Stoddard county, Mo	31
Poole's Prairie, Mo	33	Stone Mountain, Ga	10
Potean Mountain, Ark	12	Swallow's Bluff, Miss	22
Preston, Mo	33		
Pulaski county, Ga	8	Tabor Church, Ky	27
		Thomas' Station, Ga	11
Randolph's Forge, Tenn	23	Trace creek, Tenn	19
Red Mills, Ky	26	Triune, Tenn	19
Red River bridge, Tenn	19	Tyrn Springs, Tenn	19
Resaca, Ga	9		
Richland Station, Tenn	19	Union Meeting-house, Ky	28
Ringold School-house, Ky	27-28		
Rock Hill Station, Ky	19	Van Buren, Ark	12
Rockford Ledge, Tenn	17	Vera Cruz, Mo	33-34
Rockport, Mo	31	Vermillionville, La	14
Rome, Ga	9	Vernon, Tenn	19
Roswell, Ga	10	Verona, Mo	34
Rough and Ready Station, Ga	10	Victoria, Tex	15
		Vining's Station, Ga	9
St. Genevieve, Mo	31		
St. Martin's Parish, La	13	Waitsboro', Ala	29
Salado creek, Tex	15	Waitsboro', Ky	29
Salem Meeting-house, Ky	28	Waldon, Ark	12
Salisbury, N. C	8	Warsaw, Mo	31
Saltillo, Tenn	21	Washington, La	14
San Antonio, Tex	15	Washington, Ga	10
Sarcoxie, Mo	33	Washington county, Ga	8
Savannah, Tenn	21	Waterloo, Ala	22
Scatterville, Ark	31	Waverly, Tenn	19
Scott county, Ark	12	Waynesboro' road, Tenn	22
Scottsville, Ky	19	Waynesboro', Ga	11
Sebastian county, Ark	12	Webster county, Mo	33
Shanban Station, Ky	29	White's Bluff, Tenn	19
Sheppardsville, Ky	26	Will's Valley, Ala	10
Shiloh, Tenn	21-22	Winchester, Ky	29
Shiloh Church, Tenn	21-22	Wolf creek, Ky	27
Shiloh Church, Ky	28	Woodbury, Ky	19
Shirley's Ford, Mo	32	Woodsonville, Ky	26
Shreveport, La	13		
Signal Hill, Tenn	19	Ypsilanti, Mich	30

ALPHABETICAL INDEX

TO

NATIONAL CEMETERIES WHERE BODIES HAVE BEEN DEPOSITED.

	Page.		Page.
Andersonville, Ga.	8	Lawton, Ga.	11
Alexandria, La.	13	Lexington, Ky.	29
		Logan's X Roads, Ky.	27
Brownsville, Tex.	15	Louisville, (Cave Hill) Ky.	26
Cave Hill, (Louisville) Ky.	25	Marietta, Ga.	9
Chalmette, La.	13		
		Nashville, Tenn.	16
Fort Donelson, Tenn.	23		
Fort Shaw, Montana.	34	Perryville, Tenn.	23
Fort Smith, Ark.	12		
Fort Wayne, Mich.	30	Salisbury, N. C.	8
		San Antonio, Tex.	15
Galveston, Tex.	15	Shiloh, Tenn.	20
		Springfield, Mo.	31
Jefferson Barracks, Mo.	30		

STATEMENT

OF THE

DISPOSITION OF SOME OF THE BODIES

OF

DECEASED UNION SOLDIERS

AND

PRISONERS OF WAR

WHOSE REMAINS HAVE BEEN REMOVED

TO

NATIONAL CEMETERIES

IN THE SOUTHERN AND WESTERN STATES.

VOLUME IV.

"Who seem to die in such a cause,
Ye cannot call them dead."

WASHINGTON:
GOVERNMENT PRINTING OFFICE.
1869.

STATEMENT OF THE FINAL DISPOSITION OF DECEASED UNION SOLDIERS, VOL. IV.

GENERAL ORDERS } QUARTERMASTER GENERAL'S OFFICE,
No. 12. } WASHINGTON, D. C., *March* 2, 1869.

The following statement of the final disposition of some of the bodies of deceased Union Soldiers and Prisoners of War, whose remains have been removed to National Cemeteries in the Southern and Western States, prepared in this office, under the direction of Brevet Brigadier General ALEX. J. PERRY, Q. M., U. S. Army, is published by authority of the Secretary of War, for the information of surviving comrades and friends, and for use in connection with the "Rolls of Honor," heretofore published by this Office.

M. C. MEIGS,
Quartermaster General,
Brevet Major General U. S. A.

QUARTERMASTER GENERAL'S OFFICE,
WASHINGTON, D. C., *February* 20, 1869.

Brevet Major Gen. M. C. MEIGS,
Quartermaster General, U. S. A.

GENERAL:

The enclosed "Statement of the Final Disposition of the Bodies of Deceased Union Soldiers and Prisoners of War, whose remains have been removed to National Cemeteries in the Southern and Western States," is respectfully forwarded, with the request that it be printed for distribution and use in connection with the "Rolls of Honor" heretofore issued from this Office.

It is the fourth volume of this work, and embraces the removals to the National Cemeteries at Chattanooga and Nashville, Tenn., New Albany, Ind., Springfield, Mo., Fredericksburg, Staunton, Richmond, Petersburg, Hampton, and Winchester, Va.; in it is recorded the removal of sixty-three thousand eight hundred and forty-seven bodies, from two hundred and ninety-five different localities to twenty-three of the National Cemeteries.

I am, General, very respectfully,
Your obedient servant,
ALEX. J. PERRY,
Bv't Brig. Gen'l, and Q. M. U. S. A.

TABLE OF CONTENTS.

List of the States from and to which the Bodies of Deceased Union Soldiers and Prisoners of War have been removed.

No.	From places in—	To Cemeteries in—	Number of Bodies.	Page.
I.	Virginia	Virginia	42,755	1
II.	Texas	Texas	1,509	30
III.	Georgia	Georgia	2	31
IV.	Ohio	Ohio	1	31
V.	Dakota Territory	Dakota Ter.	1	31
VI.	Louisiana	Louisiana	1,978	31
VII.	Missouri	Missouri	35	32
VIII.	Tennessee, Kentucky, Alabama, Georgia, and North Carolina	Tennessee	12,292	32
IX.	Indiana, Kentucky, and Virginia	Indiana	2,788	36
X.	Kentucky	Kentucky	2,378	37
XI.	Pennsylvania	Pennsylva'a	35	37
XII.	Illinois	Illinois	73	37
	Alphabetical Index of places from which bodies have been removed			39
	Alphabetical Index of Cemeteries to which bodies have been removed			43
	Total		63,847	

I.—From places in Virginia to Virginia.

No.	Number of Graves.	NUMBER AND ORIGINAL LOCATION OF GRAVES. Original Location.	DATE O REMOVAL BODIES.	FINAL DISPOSITION OF REMAINS.	
				Number of Bodies.	Final Resting Place.
1	4	Catholic grave-yard, Bath county, Va.			
2	2	English grave-yard, Bath county, "			
3	3	Lutheran grave-yard, Bath county, "			
4	13	Bolivar, "			
5	10	Grave-yard near Bolivar, "			
6	9	Episcopal Cemetery, Bunker Hill, "			
7	7	George Briscoe's farm, Charlestown, West Va.			
8	4	Mrs. Burnett's farm, Charlestown, "			
9	14	Episcopal Cemetery, Charlestown, "			
10	10	Hedge Hill Cemetery, Charlestown, Va.			
11	3	Eli Littleton's farm, Clark county, "			
12	3	McDonald's farm, Clark county, "			
13	2	Paul Sheppard's farm, Clark county, "			
14	16	Darksville, "			
15	8	John Peacher's farm, Elkton Heights, Va.			
16	14	J. Strider's farm, Elkton Heights, "			
17	7	P. Bailey's farm, Frederick county, "			
18	25	J. L. Baker's farm, Frederick county, "			
19	18	George Baker's farm, Frederick county, "			
20	3	John Beemer's farm, Frederick county, "			
21	3	George Bell's farm, Frederick county, "			
22	6	Berry's farm, Frederick county, "			
23	5	John Blair's farm, Frederick county, "			
24	1	Mrs. Bliss' farm, Frederick county, "			
25	9	J. Bower's farm, Frederick county, "			
26	65	Isaac Bowman's farm, Frederick county, "			
27	6	A. M. Bragg's farm, Frederick county, "			
28	15	O. Brown's farm, Frederick county, "			
29	5	Burnt Factory, Frederick county, "			
30	20	J. Carter's farm, Frederick county, "			
31		Mrs. Carter's farm, Frederick county, "			

32	John Chamberlain's farm, Frederick county, Va	2		
33	Child's farm, Frederick county,	7	"	
34	S. Clark's farm, Frederick county,	3	"	
35	Clevenger's farm, Frederick county,	13	"	
36	John Cooley's farm, Frederick county,	33	"	
37	Cool Spring farm, Frederick county,	63	"	
38	W. Crawford's farm, Frederick county,	8	"	
39	D. Dinger's farm, Frederick county,	13	"	
40	Enos Dinkle's farm, Frederick county,	111	"	
41	J. H. Dinkle's farm, Frederick county,	16	"	
42	Eastern's farm, Frederick county,	10	"	
43	Eddy's farm, Frederick county,	35	"	From Sept. —, 1866, to Dec. —, 1867. ... 1,193	Winchester National Cemetery, Frederick county, Virginia.
44	W. N. Eddy's farm, Frederick county,	19	"	
45	A. P. Elwell's farm, Frederick county,	1	"	
46	Falmstock's farm, Frederick county,	1	"	
47	Frazer's farm, Frederick county,	4	"	
48	A. Funkhauser's farm, Frederick county,	6	"	
49	N. Funkhauser's farm, Frederick county,	5	"	
50	G. W. Ginn's farm, Frederick county,	25	"	
51	C. Ginn's farm, Frederick county,	17	"	
52	J. Glaze's farm, Frederick county,	5	"	
53	Griffith's farm, Frederick county,	9	"	
54	Hackwood's farm, Frederick county,	203	"	
55	Isaac Haight's farm, Frederick county,	10	"	
56	Hamilton's farm, Frederick county,	18	"	
57	J. Hard's farm, Frederick county,	9	"	
58	J. Haye's farm, Frederick county,	2	"	
59	Haymaker's farm, Frederick county,	5	"	
60	S. Heater's farm, Frederick county,	18	"	
61	Wm. Heater's farm, Frederick county,	61	"	
62	Charles Height's farm, Frederick county,	27	"	
63	M. R. Hoover's farm, Frederick county,	11	"	
64	Wm. Hyne's farm, Frederick county,	21	"	
65	C. M. Jones' farm, Frederick county,	4	"	
66	Lacey's farm, Frederick county,	2	"	
67	McCormack's farm, Frederick county,	8	"	
68	Merryman's farm, Frederick county,	7	"	
69	D. Miller's farm, Frederick county,	35	"	
70	John Newcomer's farm, Frederick county,	26	"	
71	Dr. Riley's farm, Frederick county,	10	"	
	Carried forward		1 193	

From Virginia to Virginia—Continued.

No.	Number of Graves.	NUMBER AND ORIGINAL LOCATION OF GRAVES. Original Location.	DATE OF REMOVAL OF BODIES.	FINAL DISPOSITION OF REMAINS.	
				Number of Bodies.	Final Resting Place.
		Brought forward		1,193	
72	9	W. Ritter's farm, Frederick county, Va			
73	5	C. Robinson's farm, Frederick county, "			
74	57	Rockwell's farm, Frederick county, "			
75	3	Savage's farm, Frederick county, "			
76	15	J. Schwartz's farm, Frederick county, "			
77	15	Shyrock's farm, Frederick county, "			
78	19	Shimp's farm, Frederick county, "			
79	46	Samuel Sperry's farm, Frederick county, "			
80	20	Jas. Stevenson's farm, Frederick county, "			
81	37	Levi Stickley's farm, Frederick county, "			
82	13	Stine's farm, Frederick county, "			
83	6	Stony Chapel farm, Frederick county, "			
84	4	Theophilus' farm, Frederick county, "			
85	3	Touchstone's farm, Frederick county, "			
86	3	Triplett's farm, Frederick county, "			
87	25	Wallchower's farm, Frederick county, "			
88	5	Philip Williams' farm Frederick county, "			
89	25	C. Wood's farm, Frederick county, "			
90	24	D. Wood's farm, Frederick county, "			
91	3	James Wyson's farm, Frederick county, "			
92	2	Mrs. Asher's farm, Front Royal, "			
93	12	T. N. Ashley's farm, near Front Royal, "			
94	9	H. M. Breut's farm, Front Royal, "			
95	12	W. D. Garrison's farm, Front Royal, "			
96	10	J. Grabell's farm, Front Royal, "			
97	2	Gibeon Grant's farm, near Front Royal, "			
98	5	J. Hansbury's farm, near Front Royal, "			
99	5	Isaac Kern's farm, Front Royal, "			
100	15	J. Marshall's farm, Front Royal, "			
101	7	Wm. H. Melton's farm, near Front Royal, "			

102	19	Greenwood Mills, Va	
103	7	Frank Gardner's farm, Halltown, "	
104	9	Hanson's Hill, "	
105	3	Allstadt's farm, Harper's Ferry, "	
106	325	Camp Hill, Harper's Ferry, "	
107	31	Catholic grave-yard, Harper's Ferry "	
108	4	Copeland's farm, Harper's Ferry, "	
109	20	Conrad's farm, Harper's Ferry, "	
110	19	Elkton Branch church-yard, Harper's Ferry, Va.	
111	13	Frederick's farm, Harper's Ferry, "	
112	8	Jewett's farm, Harper's Ferry, "	
113	2	Lucas' farm, Harper's Ferry, "	
114	78	Lutheran grave-yard, Harper's Ferry, "	
115	26	Methodist grave-yard, Harper's Ferry, "	
116	6	Morris' farm, Harper's Ferry, "	
117	5	Roberts' farm, Harper's Ferry, "	
118	3	Snyder's farm, Harper's Ferry, "	
119	2	Sir John's Run, Baltimore and Ohio railroad "	1,495
120	7	Little Petersburg, Va	
121	14	Little Petersburg Cemetery, "	
122	6	Lovettsville Cemetery, "	
123	17	Wm. Hill's farm, Loudon county, Va	
124	1	Colored Cemetery, Martinsburg, W. Va	
125	8	Episcopal Cemetery, Martinsburg, "	
126	240	Green Hill Cemetery, Martinsburg, W. Va.	
127	44	Lutheran grave-yard, Martinsburg, "	
128	1	Massanutton Mount, (top of,) Va	
129	21	McNeal's farm, Moorefield, W. Va	
130	13	Moorefield Cemetery, "	
131	1	Dr. Paren's, Moorefield, "	
132	3	Jos. Vanmetre's farm, Moorefield, W. Va.	
133	1	Mountain Gap, (near Little Petersburg,) Va	
134	16	Mount Carmell farm, "	
135	17	Mount Hebron Cemetery, "	
136	6	Mount Jackson Cemetery, "	
137	4	Lutheran grave yard, Newmarket, "	
138	90	Lutheran grave-yard, Newtown, "	
139	4	Pine Hill Cemetery, "	
140	1	Raisher's Woods, "	
141	4	Red Hill farm, "	
		Carried forward	2,688

From Sept. —, 1866, to Dec. —, 1867 } Winchester National Cemetery, Frederick county, Virginia.

Virginia to Virginia—Continued.

No.	Number of Graves.	NUMBER AND ORIGINAL LOCATION OF GRAVES. Original Location.	DATE OF REMOVAL OF BODIES.	FINAL DISPOSITION OF REMAINS. Number of Bodies.	Final Resting Place.
		Brought forward		2,688	
142	22	Indian Mound Cemetery, Romney, W. Va			
143	18	Michael Graham's farm, Shenandoah county, Va			
144	14	John Koontz's farm, Shenandoah county, "			
145	5	Lutheran grave-yard, Shenandoah county, "			
146	5	General Minn's farm, Shenandoah county, "			
147	24	Dr. Rice's farm, Shenandoah county, "			
148	4	V. Ripley's farm, Shenandoah county, "			
149	3	John Rupert's farm, Shenandoah county, "			
150	21	D. Stickney's farm, Shenandoah county, "			
151	61	Dr. J. R. Strayer's farm, Shepperdstown, W. Va			
152	18	Presbyterian grave-yard, Shepperdstown, "			
153	7	Selby's farm, Shepperdstown, "			
154	22	Stine's farm, Shepperdstown, "			
155	1	Springfield Cemetery, "			
156	85	Presbyterian grave-yard, Strasburg, Va			
157	13	Dr. Cail's farm, Summit Point, W. Va			
158	2	Davenport grave-yard, Summit Point, W. Va			
159	13	English Cemetery, Summit Point, "			
160	15	George Flagg's farm, Summit Point, "			
161	19	David Fry's farm, Summit Point, "			
162	17	J. B. Packett's farm, Summit Point, "			
163	9	Sherley's farm, Summit Point, "			
164	14	John Thompson's farm, Summit Point, "			
165	18	W. A. Thompson's farm, Summit Point, "			
166	11	John Washington's farm, Summit Point, "			
167	6	Chas. Whittington's farm, Summit Point, "			
168	2	Sweet Run Swamp, Va			
169	6	R. S. Leche's farm, Wade's Depot, Va			
170	3	Mrs. Bivek's farm, Warren county, "			
171	4	J. R. Richard's farm, Warren county, "			

172	4	Weaterly Chapel farm,	Va.,	
173	1	Weed's Station, P. R. R.,	"	
174	65	Burger's lot, Winchester,	"	
175	70	Episcopal grave-yard, Winchester,	"	
176	183	Lutheran grave-yard, Winchester,	"	
177	408	Methodist grave-yard, Winchester,	"	
178	3	Quaker's grave-yard, Winchester,	"	From Sept.—, 1866, to Dec. —, 1867. } 1,690
179	11	Episcopal Cemetery, Woodstock,	"	
180	10	Methodist grave-yard, Woodstock,	"	
181	8	Presbyterian grave-yard, Woodstock,	"	
182	5	Robert R. Barnes' farm,	"	
183	6	Wm. Beason's farm,	"	
184	11	Judge Belcher's farm,	"	
185	8	Chapman's farm,	"	
186	12	Mrs. Clarke's farm,	"	
187	5	Dr. R. S. Colston's farm,	"	
188	3	E. Comer's farm,	"	
189	98	Benj. Cooley's farm,	"	
190	11	Crook and Crowle's farm,	"	
191	15	Mrs. Daniels' farm,	"	
192	6	D. Deeneisis' farm,	"	
193	1	Samuel Fetzer's farm,	"	
194	80	Wm. Heming's farm,	"	
195	3	J. W. Hume's farm,	"	
196	9	J. Jackson's farm,	"	
197	10	J. Jones' farm,	"	
198	6	Mrs. John Kelly's farm,	"	
199	6	A. Keister's farm,	"	
200	4	Mrs. S. Kendrick's farm,	"	
201	5	Dr. Wm. McGuire's farm,	"	
202	14	P. Miller's farm,	"	
203	37	James Myer's farm,	"	
204	2	Patterson's farm,	"	
205	39	A. Pritchard's farm,	"	
206	1	Samuel Ridgeway's farm,	"	
207	4	B. Ritchen's farm,	"	
208	44	Stephenson's farm,	"	
209	13	J. Thompson's farm,	"	
210	5	Trussell's farm,	"	
211	2	D. White's farm,	"	
		Carried forward		4,378

Winchester National Cemetery, Frederick county, Virginia.

Virginia to Virginia—Continued.

No.	Number and Original Location of Graves.		Date of Removal of Bodies.	Final Disposition of Remains.	
	Number of Graves.	Original Location.		Number of Bodies.	Final Resting Place.
		Brought forward.............		4,378	
212	7	G. P. Wills' farm, Va.............	From Sept. —, 1866, to Dec. —, 1867.	7	Winchester National Cemetery, Frederick county, Virginia.
		Total removed to Winchester, Va.....		4,385	
1	1	Bowers' Hill, Va.............			
2	2	Camp Hamilton, Va.............			
3	1	Charles City, "			
4	1	Cherrystone, "			
5	60	Craney Island, "			
6	1	Fort Monroe Hospital, Va.....			
7	1	Fort Norfolk, "			
8	33	Gettie's Station, "			
9	2	Oak Grove Church, near Great Bridge, Va			
10	3,324	Original Cemetery at Hampton, "			
11	6	Hodges' farm, near Hampton, "			
12	16	Jamestown Island, "			
13	74	Naval Hospital, "			
14	11	Newport News, "			
15	468	Norfolk Cemetery, "			
16	1	Catholic grave-yard, Norfolk, "			
17	.5	Intrenched Camp, Norfolk, "			
18	304	Portsmouth Cemetery, "			
19	1	Near Portsmouth, "			
20	3	Sawyer's Lane, (36 miles from Norfolk,) "			
21	18	Seaboard and Roanoke railroad, "			
22	1	Smithfield, "			
23	1	South Mills, "			

13

				Hampton National Cemetery, Va.
24	1	Ebenezar Church-yard, near South Mills, Va.		
25	2	Abbott's grave-yard, near South Mills, "		
26	187	Suffolk Cemetery, "		
27	7	Episcopal Church-yard, Suffolk, "		
28	15	J. Hall's farm, near Suffolk, "		
29	1	Kitteral's farm, near Suffolk, "		
30	1	3 miles from Kitteral's farm, Suffolk, "		
31	1	Muskrat farm, Suffolk, "	From June 27, to Nov. —, '67.	4,591
32	1	Sleepy Hole farm, 15 miles from Suffolk, "		
33	1	H. E. Smith's farm, Suffolk, "		
34	1	A. Stationer's farm, Suffolk, "		
35	1	Whitehall, "		
36	1	J. Barnard's farm, "		
37	1	J. E. Barnwell's yard, "		
38	5	F. Cherry's farm, "		
39	3	Durkins' farm, "		
40	1	Duck's farm, "		
41	1	J. C. Duval's farm, "		
42	1	W. E. Edwards' farm, "		
43	2	Kelley's farm, "		
44	4	Samuel Wilson's farm, "		
45	1	Wm. Lewis' farm, "		
46	8	Dr. Wright's farm, "		
47	3	Under bunch of walnut and oak trees, "		
		Total removed to Hampton, Va.		4,591
				Poplar Grove National Cemetery, Petersburg, Virginia.
1	13	Adams' farm Va.		
2	1	Aldridge farm, Va. "		
3	2	Alley's (H.) farm, Va. "		
4	3	Amelia Court-house, Va. "		
5	1	Anderson farm, Amelia C. H., Va.	From July —, 1866, to Nov. —, 1867.	281
6	35	Appomattox C. H., "		
7	42	Armstrong farm. "		
8	47	Atkins' farm, "		
9	122	Avery's farm, "		
10	2	Baldwin farm, "		
11	12	Banks' farm, "		
12	1	Bass farm, "		
		Carried forward.		281

Virginia to Virginia—Continued.

No.	NUMBER AND ORIGINAL LOCATION OF GRAVES.		DATE OF REMOVAL OF BODIES.	FINAL DISPOSITION OF REMAINS.	
	Number of Graves.	Original Location.		Number of Bodies.	Final Resting Place.
		Brought forward........		281	
13	1	Beardsley farm, Va......			
14	1	Bedford farm, "			
15	1	Major Belcher's farm, Va.......			
16	1	Bermuda Hundred, "			
17	1	Blandford School-house, Va......			
18	26	Blandford Cemetery, "			
19	87	Blick's farm, "			
20	10	Boiseau farm, "			
21	170	Dr. Boiseau's farm, "			
22	11	J. Boiseau's farm, "			
23	5	Branch farm, "			
24	3	Bryant's farm, "			
25	2	Budd's farm, "			
26	81	Burgess Mill "			
27	17	Burgess farm, "			
28	2	Burke's farm, "			
29	46	Burksville Junction, "			
30	11	Burch's farm, "			
31	6	Buther's farm, "			
32	1	Butler's farm, "			
33	51	Choakley's farm, "			
34	1	Mrs. Clark's farm, "			
35	10	Clemmens' farm, "			
36	3	Cobb's farm, "			
37	3	Cogswell's farm, "			
38	1	Comer's farm, "			
39	4	Conway's farm, "			
40	669	Crater, "			
41	1	Crowley's farm, "			
42	175	Cummings' farm, "			

43	Dabney's farm,	88	Va.	
44	Dabney's Mill,	109	"	
45	Damnation, (Fort,)	1	"	
46	Davis, (Fort,)	16	"	
47	Davis' farm,	95	"	
48	Delaney's farm,	1	"	
49	Deply's farm,	2	"	
50	Dutch Gap,	1	"	
51	Ellis farm,	4	"	
52	Ennis farm,	1	"	
53	Eommon's farm,	3	"	
54	Evergreen farm,	2	"	
55	Fair Ground, near Petersburg, Va.	113		
56	Farley's farm,	5	"	
57	Farmville,	75	"	
58	Farrell's farm,	2	"	
59	Mrs. Finn's farm,	47	"	
60	Fisher's farm,	4	"	
61	Fitzgerald's farm,	2	"	
62	Five Forks,	123	"	
63	Flowers' farm,	192	"	
64	Freeman's farm,	2	"	
65	Friend's farm,	35	"	
66	Gatton's (Amelia C. H.,)	1	"	
67	Gilliam's farm,	17	"	
68	Gill's farm,	7	"	
69	Captain Goodwin's farm,	2	"	
70	Gravelly Church,	13	"	
71	Gregg, (Fort,)	126	"	
72	Gregg's farm,	2	"	
73	Gregory farm,	9	"	
74	Dr. Gurley's farm,	67	"	
75	Hancock Station,	3	"	
76	Hank's farm,	1	"	
77	Dr. Hardway's,	2	"	
78	Hargrave farm,	2	"	
79	Harper farm, Sailors' Creek,	12	"	
80	Harrison's Landing,	27	"	
81	J. Harrison's farm,	3	"	
82	Hart's farm,	12	"	
	Carried forward			2,650 } From July —, 1866, to Nov. —, 1867. Poplar Grove National Cemetery, Petersburg, Virginia. 2,931

Virginia to Virginia—Continued.

No.	Number and Original Location of Graves.		Date of Removal of Bodies.	Final Disposition of Remains.	
	Number of Graves.	Original Location.		Number of Bodies.	Final Resting Place.
		Brought forward		2,931	
83	4	Haskins, (Fort,) Va.,			
84	9	Hatcher's Run, "			
85	11	Hatcher's farm, "			
86	212	Hell, (Fort,) "			
87	45	Mrs. Hillman's farm, Sailors' Creek, Va.			
88	20	Howlett's farm, "			
89	3	Howlett's Gate, Amelia Court-house, "			
90	1	Jackson Mill, "			
91	2	Jettersville, "			
92	17	Jones' House, "			
93	39	Jones' farm, "			
94	5	Jourdan farm, "			
95	3	Mrs. Keer's farm, "			
96	3	Lanier's farm, "			
97	76	Lewis' farm, "			
98	5	J. Lewis' farm, "			
99	6	Liberty Church, "			
100	9	Lockett's farm, "			
101	9	Longworth farm, "			
102	260	Lynchburg farm, "			
103	2	McCann's farm, "			
104	1	Marshall farm, "			
105	684	Mead's Station, "			
106	4	Widow Miller's farm, "			
107	1	Miller's farm, "			
108	12	Mumford farm, "			
109	1	Nash farm, "			
110	1	Nazomie Church, "			
111	2	Newman farm, "			
112	8	W. Norris farm, "			

No.		Location	State		Total
113	1	Norton farm,	Va.		
114	6	Oak Grove,	"		
115	3	Osborne farm,	"		
116	1	Parmetory farm,	"		
117	55	Peble's farm,	"		
118	8	O. Pegram's farm.	"		
119	2	Pendexter farm,	"		
120	6	Perdie's farm,	"		
121	10	Dr. Perkins' farm,	"		
122	2	Perkinson's farm,	"		
123	4	Pierce's farm,	"		
124	10	Poplar Grove Cemetery,	"		
125	8	Poplar Grove Lawn,	"		
126	2	Presbyterian Church,	"		
127	15	Mrs. Rainey's farm,	"		
128	123	Ream Station,	"		
129	2	Reed's farm,	"		
130	7	T. Reed's farm,	"		
131	5	Rice Station,	"		
132	5	Rice's farm,	"		
133	3	Robinson farm,	"		
134	5	N. Roth's farm,	"		
135	1	Roth farm,	"		
136	1	Rowland farm,	"		
137	4	Royal farm,	"		
138	6	Safrona Church,	"		
139	4	Scott's farm,	"		
140	24	Sidney farm,	"		
141	7	Smith farm,	"		
142	1	I. Smith's farm,	"		
143	3	Snider farm,	"		
144	28	Smithall farm,	"		
145	7	Snyd's farm,	"		
146	1	Spain's,	"		
147	4	Spier's farm,	"		
148	186	Steadman, (Fort,)	"		
149	118	Steadman, (Fort,) (in front of,)	"		
150	1	Stony Creek,	"		
151	3	Sussex Court-house,	"		
152	26	Sutherland Station,	"		

Poplar Grove National Cemetery, Petersburg, Virginia. 2,163

From July —, 1866, to Nov. —, 1867.

Carried forward 5,094

Virginia to Virginia—Continued.

No.	Number of Graves.	NUMBER AND ORIGINAL LOCATION OF GRAVES. Original Location†	DATE OF REMOVAL OF BODIES.	FINAL DISPOSITION OF REMAINS.	
				Number of Bodies.	Final Resting Place.
		Brought forward		5,094	
153	55	Talmadge farm, Va			
154	38	W. B. Taylor's farm, Va			
155	37	Taylor farm, "			
156	28	Temple farm, "			
157	3	Thompson farm, "			
158	1	Tompkins' farm, "			
159	7	Warren Station, "			
160	32	Watkins', (Bermuda Hundred,) Va.			
161	10	Watson farm, Rice Station, "	From July —, 1866, to Nov. —, 1867.	453	Poplar Grove National Cemetery, Petersburg, Virginia.
162	149	Webb's farm, "			
163	28	Westbrook farm, "			
164	3	Widdle farm, "			
165	4	Widdlefare farm, "			
166	2	Wilkinson's farm, "			
167	30	Willis' farm, "			
168	11	Williams' farm, "			
169	9	Wilson farm, "			
170	5	Woolsick farm, "			
171	1	Captain Wyatt's farm, "			
		Total removed to Petersburg, Va		5,547	
1	970	Cold Harbor, (battlefield,) Va			
2	82	Mr. Mount Castle's farm, "			
3	428	Richmond City Hospital, "			
4	5	Sharp's Cemetery, Richmond, Va			
5	211	Vicinity of Cold Harbor, "			
6	227	Bell Island, (James River,) "			
7	1,432	Oakwood Cemetery, Richmond, Va			

8	9	J. A. Eacho's farm, Va.		
9	896	Hollywood Cemetery, Richmond, "		
10	13	Savage Station, "		
11	6	Hungry Station, "		
12	11	Liberty Hall, (Hanover county,) "		
13	6	Cartersfield, near Mechanicsville, "		
14	29	Mechanicsville, "		
15	3	Henrico county, "		
16	393	Hanover county, "		
17	48	Pole Green Church, "		
18	10	Mary Wier's farm, "		
19	4	Charles City Road, "		
20	1	Ground Squirrel Bridge, "		
21	15	Beaver Dam Station, "		
22	6	J. Fountain's farm, "		
23	5	Dr. Andrew's farm, "		
24	2	Dr. Rowzier's farm, "		
25	5	Munley's Mill, "	From Sept. 1, 1866, to Sept. 30, 1867.	5,896	Richmond National Cemetery, Va.
26	1	P. Butler's farm, "		
27	207	Near Fort Harrison, "		
28	128	Vicinity of Richmond Poorhouse, "		
29	558	Miles Gathmight's farm, "		
30	1	Chaff's farm, near Griffin's Spring, Va.		
31	3	Williams' farm, "		
32	8	Near Williamsburg Road, "		
33	29	White Oak Swamp, "		
34	26	Dr. Garnett's farm, "		
35	4	In a creek near Fredericks Hall Station, Va.		
36	6	Shaw's farm, "		
37	8	Colored Cemetery at Rocketts, "		
38	4	Day's farm, "		
39	15	Near Gordonsville, "		
40	4	Stanley's farm, "		
41	10	Madder's farm "		
42	7	Green's farm, "		
43	7	Dabney's farm, "		
44	18	Hanover Junction, "		
45	22	Johnson's farm, "		
46	2	Allen's farm, "		
47	11	Rodman's farm, "		
		Carried forward		5,896

Virginia to Virginia—Continued.

No.	NUMBER AND ORIGINAL LOCATION OF GRAVES.		DATE OF REMOVAL OF BODIES.	FINAL DISPOSITION OF REMAINS.	
	Number of Graves.	Original Location.		Number of Bodies.	Final Resting Place.
		Brought forward		5,996	
48	7	Darling's farm, Va.			
49	4	Easterbrook's farm, Va.			
50	6	Jackson's farm, "			
51	6	Nevil's farm, "			
52	3	Fair Oak Station, "			
53	21	Savage's farm, "			
54	73	Bottom's Bridge, "			
55	27	Tom Carter's farm, "			
56	17	Wein's farm, "	From Sept. 1, 1866, to Sept. 30, 1867.	405	Richmond National Cemetery, Va.
57	14	Taylor's farm, "			
58	43	Childrey's farm, "			
59	15	Griner's farm, "			
60	16	A. Childrey's farm, "			
61	34	Trockmorton's farm, "			
62	39	New Kent and Charles City Road, (junction,) Va.			
63	9	Whiteside's farm, "			
64	9	Ames' farm, "			
65	15	Seven Pines, "			
66	13	Half-way House, R. and P. turnpike, "			
67	34	Miner's farm, "			
		Total removed to Richmond, Va.		6,301	
1	2,739	City Point, Va.			
2	2,165	Point of Rocks, Va.			
3	23	Ruffin's plantations, Va.	From July —, 1866, to Sept. —, 1867.	5,123	City Point National Cemetery, Va.
4	62	Banks of Appomattox, near B. Way's Landing, Va.			
5	111	Banks of Appomattox, near Lepsey's House, "			
6	23	Meade Station, "			

		Total removed to City Point, Va............		5,123	
1		Rebel prison at Danville, Va............	} From Dec. —, 1866, to May —, 1868.	1,316	Danville National Cemetery, Va.
1	19	A. Perkey's farm, near Harrisburg, Va............			
2	59	B. Crawford's farm, near Piedmont, "			
3	32	General John Lewis' farm, near Port Republic, Va.			
4	59	Thornrose Cemetery, Staunton, "			
5	16	Presbyterian Church grave-yard, Harrisburg, "			
6	13	Town Cemetery, Harrisburg, "			
7	5	Samuel Gardner's farm, "			
8	12	David Tualey's farm, "			
9	51	Myers' Woods, "			
10	40	Walker's Woods, "			
11	8	J. H. Tost's farm, "			
12	1	L. Garrison's Pasture, "	} From Nov. —, 1866, to Dec. —, 1867.	571	Staunton National Cemetery, Va.
13	1	Asylum Hill, "			
14	1	Joseph Peters' farm, "			
15	11	James Patterson's farm, "			
16	1	Henry Rexroad's farm, "			
17	1	John Brown's farm, "			
18	1	J. R. Steward's farm, "			
19	3	Mrs. Mittenberger's farm, "			
20	95	Kennedy's farm, "			
21	2	Pumphrey's farm, "			
22	2	Lincoln's farm, "			
23	14	H. Miller's farm, "			
24	2	Oakland Church-yard, "			
25	82	Franklin Cemetery, "			
26	26	John Miller's farm, "			
27	2	M. E. Church grave-yard, "			
28	1	P. Long's farm, "			
29	7	Goodwin's farm, "			
30	1	Williams' farm, "			
31	1	L. Shaver's farm, "			
32	2	J. Good's farm, "			
		Carried forward............		571	

Virginia to Virginia—Continued.

No.	NUMBER AND ORIGINAL LOCATION OF GRAVES.		DATE OF REMOVAL OF BODIES.	FINAL DISPOSITION OF REMAINS.	
	Number of Graves.	Original Location.		Number of Bodies.	Final Resting Place.
		Brought forward		571	
33	1	Allebaugh's farm, Va.			
34	7	Lurry C. H. grave-yard, Va.			
35	1	Yates' farm, "			
36	8	T. H. Henning's farm. "			
37	5	J. E. Bell's farm, "			
38	4	R. Goodrich's farm, "			
39	1	Hendricks' farm, "			
40	13	F. Stockton's farm, "			
41	1	Mrs. Orgabright's Woods, Va.			
42	17	White Sulphur Spring Ground, Va.			
43	6	Geo. W. Effinger's farm,			
44	1	Ellen Morris' farm, "	From Nov. —, 1866, to Dec. —, 1867.	177	Staunton National Cemetery, Va.
45	1	Ott's farm, "			
46	1	Samuel Parm's farm, "			
47	1	James Bush's farm, "			
48	1	Johnson's farm, "			
49	3	B. Hinkley's farm, "			
50	8	J. G. Bell's farm, "			
51	1	C. S. Weaver's Orchard, "			
52	2	Samuel Carpenter's farm, "			
53	2	Hooke's Woods, "			
54	2	Kemper's farm, "			
55	1	Brook's farm, "			
56	2	Jackson River Depot, "			
57	1	Aman's Woods, "			
58	1	Lacey's Spring, "			
59	7	Feyette C. H. Cemetery, "			
60	26	J. M. Platt's, jr., farm, "			
61	1	J. Schular's farm, "			
62	1	W. Coxe's farm, "			

23

63	1	Monterey Highland Company, Va.	
64	1	F. Callahant's farm, "	
65	5	Union Church-yard, "	
66	10	Kennard's farm, "	
67	3	John Garst's farm, "	
68	1	J. G. Vygal's farm, "	
69	12	S. Flory's farm, "	
70	1	Salem Toll-gate Company, "	
71	1	Kerrin's farm, "	
72	5	Wm. Sharp's farm, "	
73	1	P. S. Brown's farm, "	
74	1	P. Hinton's farm, "	
75	1	Manuel's Church Cemetery, "	
76	2	H. P. Hershberger's farm, "	
77	1	P. A. Carrall's yard, "	
78	1	Furey's Furnace, Page county, "	
79	1	Mrs. R. Barbour's farm, "	
80	1	Jacob Bowers' farm, "	
81	1	Cloyd's Mountain, "	
		Total removed to Staunton, Va.	748
1	76	Pratt's farm, Va.	
2	1,279	Chancellorsville, Va.	
3	274	Laurel Hill, "	
4	5	Stewart's farm, "	
5	71	Camback's Mill, "	Fredericksburg National Cemetery, Va. From Dec. —, 1866, to July 30, 1868.
6	3	Campbell's farm, "	
7	1	Collins' farm, "	
8	2	Swan's farm, "	
9	1	Wyman's farm, "	
10	1,464	Lively's farm, "	
11	13	McCool's farm, "	
12	4	Landrum's farm, "	
13	3,148	Massaponax Church, Va.	
14	106	Wilderness battle-field, Va.	
15	40	Wilderness Dale farm, "	
16	36	Chancellor's tract, "	
17		Geo. Chancellor's farm, "	6,526
		Carried forward	6,526

Virginia to Virginia—Continued.

No.	NUMBER AND ORIGINAL LOCATION OF GRAVES.		DATE OF REMOVAL OF BODIES.	FINAL DISPOSITION OF REMAINS.	
	Number of Graves.	Original Location.		Number of Bodies.	Final Resting Place.
		Brought forward		6,526	
18	133	Lacey's farm, Va			
19	71	O'Brannon's farm, Va			
20	379	Heverley's farm, "			
21	295	Allsop's farm, "			
22	170	Harris' farm, "			
23	25	Fox's farm, "			
24	10	Wellford's farm, "			
25	13	Talley's farm, "			
26	35	Bulloch's farm, "			
27	6	Grady's farm, "			
28	509	Lanford's farm, "			
29	26	Bibb's farm, "			
30	56	Pollock's farm, "			
31	72	Hart's farm, "			
32	1	Goodman's farm, "			
33	6	Peabody's farm, "			
34	43	Gales' farm, "			
35	13	Streshley's farm, "			
36	34	Robinson's farm, "			
37	30	Jones' farm, "			
38	8	Frazer's farm, "			
39	4	John Ander's farm, "			
40	24	A. Cliff's farm, "			
41	10	Hansford's farm, "			
42	15	Coase's farm, "			
43	171	Morrison's farm, "			
44	227	Phillips' farm, "			
45	129	Brown's farm, "			
46	706	Fredericksburg Fair Grounds, Va			
47	29	Ely's Ford, "			

48	Hicks' farm,	Va.		
49	4	Mrs. Carter's farm,	"	
50	35	Baldwin's farm,	"	
51	32	Pritchett's farm,	"	
52	28	Centre Branch Hospital,	"	
53	85	Wilderness Cemetery No. 2.	"	
54	200	Robert Lee's farm,	"	From Dec. —, 1866, to July 30, 1868. 5,002
55	24	Spottsylvania Court-house,	"	
56	39	Butler's farm,	"	
57	16	John Montheith's farm,	"	
58	21	Nancy Green's farm,	"	
59	153	White Oak Church,	"	
60	52	Fletcher Chapel's lot,	"	
61	20	G. P. King's farm,	"	
62	24	Ball's farm,	"	
63	29	Aldridge's farm,	"	
64	7	John Perry's farm,	"	
65	84	Allen's farm,	"	
66	45	Sullivan's farm,	"	
67	49	A. Wallace's farm,	"	
68	151	Bray's farm,	"	
69	15	Hansborough's farm,	"	
70	20	Shelton's farm,	"	
71	28	Old Church lot,	"	
72	2	A. Rowe's farm,	"	
73	50	Randall's farm,	"	
74	11	Sand's farm,	"	
75	1	Hoffman's farm,	"	
76	29	Miss A. Fitzhugh's farm,	"	
77	250	Luck's farm,	"	
78	3	Hayes' farm,	"	
79	2	Anderson's farm,	"	
80	104	McCarty's farm,	"	
81	7	Rollin's farm,	"	
82	6	Heurkamp's farm,	"	
83	1	Joseph Chinus' farm,	"	
84	10	Primmer's farm,	"	
85	79	Salvington farm,	"	
86	11	Bradshaw farm,	"	
87	16	Belle Plain farm,	"	
	9	Carried forward		11,528

Virginia to Virginia—Continued.

No.	Number of Graves.	NUMBER AND ORIGINAL LOCATION OF GRAVES.		DATE OF REMOVAL OF BODIES.	FINAL DISPOSITION OF REMAINS.	
		Original Location			Number of Bodies.	Final Resting Place.
		Brought forward			11,528	
88	20	Casey's farm, Va.,				
89	25	Joseph Williams' farm, Va.,				
90	7	Lang's farm,	"			
91	8	John Berry's farm,	"			
92	6	Kent's farm,	"			
93	10	Spindle's farm,	"			
94	46	Goolrick's lot,	"			
95	42	Fredericksburg ice-house, Va.,				
96	67	Mrs. R. Smith's farm,	"			
97	328	Charles Miller's lot,	"			
98	1	Kendal's lot,	"			
99	1	J. H. Bradley's lot,	"			
100	21	Masonic Cemetery, Fredericksburg, Va.,				
101	1	Buckner's farm,	"			
102	1	A. Scott's lot,	"			
103	2	Genther's lot,	"			
104	19	Mrs. Gray's farm,	"			
105	3	Allison's farm,	"			
106	1	Knight's farm,	"			
107	1	Henry Bird's farm,	"			
108	23	Adams' farm,	"			
109	4	Myers' farm,	"			
110	139	Woolen Factory lot,	"			
111	2	John Caldwell's lot,	"			
112	2	River's lot,	"			
113	1	James Walker's lot,	"			
114	4	Mrs. Fitzgerald's lot,	"			
115	2	Reynolds' lot,	"			
116	20	Mrs. Coon's farm,	"			
117	3	Stanard's lot,	"			

118	Hazlett's lot,	3	Va.	
119	Roy's lot,	103	"	
120	Arnatt's lumber yard,	16	"	
121	Mrs. Neal's lot,	18	"	
122	Marye's Heights,	19	"	
123	Kenmore House,	100	"	
124	Freedmens' Hospital,	44	"	
125	African Church lot,	1	"	
126	Mrs. Kelley's lot,	8	"	
127	Baptist Church,	2	"	
128	Falmouth grave-yard,	59	"	
129	Haydon's lot,	14	"	
130	Bernard's farm,	146	"	From Dec. —, 1866, to July 30, 1868. } 1,711 Fredericksburg National Cemetery, Va.
131	Mrs. Downman's farm,	2	"	
132	Salem Church lot,	91	"	
133	Clifford's farm,	1	"	
134	Holmes' lot,	38	"	
135	Little's lot,	14	"	
136	Fredericksburg Cemetery,	26	"	
137	Mitchell's farm,	3	"	
138	Blakie's farm,	2	"	
139	Howard's farm,	1	"	
140	Baston's farm,	5	"	
141	Post Hospital,	2	"	
142	Fall Hill's farm,	21	"	
143	Mount Carmell Church,	1	"	
144	Rix's farm,	22	"	
145	Worham's farm,	3	"	
146	Mathew's farm,	23	"	
147	James Fountain's farm,	31	"	
148	Doswell's farm,	37	"	
149	Hackett's farm,	3	"	
150	Thomas Chandler's farm,	5	"	
151	James Thomas' farm,	12	"	
152	Wm. B. Blunt's farm,	1	"	
153	P. Burrough's farm,	4	"	
154	W. Pemberton's farm,	1	"	
155	Moncure's farm,	5	"	
156	Cady's farm,	3	"	
157	Lowery's farm,	11	"	
	Carried forward			13,239

Virginia to Virginia—Continued.

No.	Number of Graves.	NUMBER AND ORIGINAL LOCATION OF GRAVES. Original Location.	DATE OF REMOVAL OF BODIES.	FINAL DISPOSITION OF REMAINS.	
				Number of Bodies.	Final Resting Place.
		Brought forward		13,239	
153	4	Novell's farm, Va			
154	1	Belle View farm, Va			
160	1	Leyton's lot, "			
161	1	Mill Race farm, "			
162	4	Cross farm, "			
163	45	Stafford C. H., "			
164	98	Douglass farm, "			
165	9	Washington farm "			
166	112	Brooks' Station, "			
167	43	Mine Run, "			
168	22	Hope Landing, "			
169	7	Graves' farm, "			
170	6	Bullard's farm, "			
171	1	Daffin's farm, "			
172	21	Bruce's farm, "			
173	230	Marlboro' Point, "			
174	37	Alexander's farm, "			
175	46	Tump's farm, "			
176	8	Aquia Creek, "			
177	71	Hedgeman's farm, Va			
178	2	Aquia Church, "			
179	8	Hervison's farm, "			
180	40	Wroten's farm, "			
181	13	Episcopal Church-yard, Va			
182	9	Potter's field, "			
183	31	Douglass Gordon's lot, "			
184	36	Old Methodist Cemetery, "			
185	49	Cook's farm, "			
186	46	Locust Grove, "			
187	1	Grasci's farm, "			

188	1	Cash's lot,	Va.			Fredericksburg National Cemetery, Va.
189	91	Henry' farm,	"			
190	21	Mackey's farm,	"			
191	8	Tyson's farm,	"			
192	12	Cunningham's farm,	"			
193	4	Heartwood Cemetery,	"			
194	9	Irwin's farm,	"			
195	4	Kellog's farm,	"			
196	25	Schooler's farm,	"	From Dec. —, 1866, to July 30, 1868.	1,497	
197	101	Arnold's farm,	"			
198	6	R. Stevens' farm,	"			
199	15	Colter's farm,	"			
200	6	Ireland's farm,	"			
201	15	Rowley's farm,	"			
202	8	Guy's farm,	"			
203	3	G. Waller's farm,	"			
204	1	Armstrong's farm,	"			
205	4	John Green's farm,	"			
206	11	Taylor's farm,	"			
207	1	Todd's farm,	"			
208	1	McGregor's farm,	"			
209	3	Dr. Smith's farm,	"			
210	13	Gallahorn's farm,	"			
211	2	Mrs. Skincker's farm,	"			
212	76	Dabney's farm,	"			
213	2	Flippo's farm,	"			
214	1	Stanley's farm,	"			
215	7	Dr. McKenney's farm,	"			
216	2	T. Towson's farm,	"			
217	4	W. Slaughter's farm,	"			
218	3	F. Slaughter's farm,	"			
219	1	Peyton's lot,	"			
220	1	Cox's lot,	"			
221	1	Conche's farm,	"			
222	20	Port Royal,	"			
223	1	Grimes' farm,	"			
224	7	Warsaw Church lot,	"			
225	2	Union Wharf,	"			
226	1	Rose Hill Point,	"			
227	1	Westmoreland C. H,	"			
		Carried forward.			14,736	

Virginia to Virginia—Concluded.

No.	Number and Original Location of Graves.		Date of Removal of Bodies.	Final Disposition of Remains.	
	Original Location.	Number of Graves.		Number of Bodies.	Final Resting Place.
	Brought forward..................			14,736	
228	Captain Pierson's farm, Va.........	2	From Dec. —, 1866, to July 30, 1868.	7	Fredericksburg National Cemetery, Va.
229	Lightfoot's farm, "	1			
230	Trap's farm, "	1			
231	Caroline county, "	1			
232	Packard's farm, "	1			
233	Jennings' Old Field, "	1			
	Total removed to Fredericksburg, Va.....			14,743	

II.—From places in Texas to Texas.

No.	Original Location.	Number of Graves.	Date of Removal of Bodies.	Number of Bodies.	Final Resting Place.
1	Hospital Burying Ground, Edinburg, Texas.....	39	From Jan 27, to July 4, 1868.	1,509	Brownsville National Cemetery, Texas.
2	Cortinas Ranch, "	1			
3	Rancho Blanco, "	6			
4	Barrancas, "	2			
5	Santa Maria, "	4			
6	Post Hospital at Brownsville, "	759			
7	Fort Brown, Brownsville, "	1			
8	Unknown Cemetery near Brownsville, "	156			
9	Plazo on Government Reservation, Brownsville, Texas..				
10	White's Ranch, "	8			
11	Brazos, Santiago, "	45			
12	Clarksville, "	446			
13	City Cemetery at Brownsville, "	30			
14	Near Cavalry Barracks, "	3			
		9			

III.—From places in Georgia to Georgia.

		Place disinterred from	Date		Place reinterred at
1	1	Cathedral Cemetery, Savannah, Ga..........	March 13, 1865	1	Laurel Grove Cemetery, Savannah, Ga.
2	1	Near A. I. Hansell's house, Marietta, Ga.	July 22, 1868	1	Marietta Cemetery, Ga.

IV.—From Ohio to Ohio.

| 1 | 1 | West side Cemetery, Cleveland, Ohio | July 3, 1868 | 1 | Woodland Cemetery, Cleveland, Ohio. |

V.—From Dakota Territory to Dakota Territory.

| 1 | 1 | Brûle Creek, D. T. | April 16, 1868 | 1 | Fort Dakota, D. T. |

VI.—From places in Louisiana to Louisiana.

1	15	Outside Cemetery at Baton Rouge, La.	July 24, 1868	15	Square 32, Baton Rouge National Cemetery, Louisiana.
2	21	John Rist's farm,	"		
3	9	Woods near Port Hudson,	"		
4	201	Mrs. Montagudo's farm,	"		
5	1	Point Coupee,	"	From April 3, 1868, to July 27, 1868.	1,963	Port Hudson National Cemetery, La
6	1,191	Vicinity of Cemetery Port Hudson,	"		
7	146	Mount Pleasant Landing,	"		
8	194	Near Jackson Sally Port,	"		
9	100	Captain Griffith's farm,	"		
10	100	Albert Nevill's farm,	"		
		Total....................		1,978	

31

VII.—From places in Missouri to Missouri.

No.	Number and Original Location of Graves.		Date of Removal of Bodies.	Final Disposition of Remains.	
	Number of Graves.	Original Location.		Number of Bodies.	Final Resting Place.
1	2	Near Elk's Mills, McDonald county, Mo.	From June 29 to July 14, '63.	35	Springfield National Cemetery, Mo.
2	1	Esquire Williams' farm, McDonald county, Mo.			
3	1	Von Pohl's farm, McDonald county, "			
4	2	Mr. Shields' farm, McDonald county, "			
5	1	Mr. Fields' farm, McDonald county, "			
6	2	Hiram Baker's farm, McDonald county, "			
7	1	Near D. Harmon's farm, McDonald county, "			
8	1	Blairley's farm, McDonald county, "			
9	1	Moore's farm, McDonald county, "			
10	1	Green Prairies, Green county, "			
11	1	Near Springfield, Green county, "			
12	3	Mr. Terrin's farm, Polk county, "			
13	1	Mr. Perryman's farm, Polk county, "			
14	1	Public Cemetery, Bolivar, "			
15	3	Public Cemetery, Mount Gilead, "			
16	2	Mr. Murray's farm, "			
17	2	Dallas county, "			
18	3	Mr. Crudenight's farm, "			
19	1	North bank of Pomme de Terre Creek, "			
20	1	South bank of Pomme de Terre Creek, "			
21	4	Mr. Horton's farm, "			
22	2	Mr. Cox's farm, "			

VIII.—From places in Tennessee, Kentucky, Alabama, Georgia, and North Carolina, to Tennessee.

1	5,418	Chattanooga, Tenn.			
2	301	Bridgeport, Ala.			
3	22	Mission Ridge, Tenn.			
4	2	Lookout Mountain, Tenn.			
5	698	Resaca, Ga.			
6	18	Crawfords, Ga.			
7	90	Ringgold, "			

33

Chattanooga National Cemetery, Tenn.

9,501

9,501

Comprising original interments and bodies transferred previous to the adoption of Field Records.

8	Chickamauga, Tenn	197
9	Stevenson, Ala	66
10	Carpenters, "	19
11	Shell Mound, Tenn	11
12	Dalton, Ga	156
13	Cleveland, Tenn	22
14	Philadelphia, Tenn	2
15	Tunnel Hill, Ga	23
16	Whiteside, Tenn	5
17	Ooltawah, "	6
18	London, "	38
19	Roseville, Ga	4
20	Atlanta, "	2
21	Wells Valley, R. R., Ga	1
22	Graysville, "	8
23	Cumberland Mountain, Tenn	7
24	Tantalon, "	2
25	Granville, "	1
26	Battle Creek, Ala	3
27	Marietta, Ga	2
28	Lee's Mills, Ga	1
29	Athens, Tenn	4
30	Charleston, Tenn	2
31	Senior Station, Tenn	3
32	David's Cross-roads, Tenn	3
33	Kingston, "	9
34	Anderson, "	2
35	Kelly's Ferry, "	2
36	Jasper, "	3
37	Cloud Spring, "	2
38	Suck Creek, "	1
39	Fort Hill, near Bridgeport, Ala	6
40	Rocky Ford, Ga	1
41	Roache's farm, "	1
42	Near Stringer's Hill, Ga	1
43	Near Jack Stringer's, "	1
44	Near Williams' Island, Ga	1
45	Tracy City, "	1
46	Sweetwater, "	1
47	Unknown	
	Carried forward	2,337

Tennessee, &c.—Concluded.

No.	NUMBER AND ORIGINAL LOCATION OF GRAVES.		FINAL DISPOSITION OF REMAINS.		
	Number of Graves.	Original Location.	DATE OF REMOVAL OF BODIES.	Number of Bodies.	Final Resting Place.
		Brought forward		9,501	
48	182	Huntsville and vicinity, Ala.	Nov. —, 1866		
49	315	Huntsville and vicinity, "	Dec. —, 1866		
50	135	Huntsville and vicinity, "	Jan. —, 1867		
51	22	Huntsville and vicinity, "	Feb. —, 1867		
52	997	Post Hospital, Chattanooga, Tenn.	Feb. to July,'67		
53	120	Chickamauga and vicinity, "	May to Nov.,'67		
54	9	Lookout Mountain, "	May —, 1867		
55	101	Jackson and Madison counties, Tenn.	May —, 1867		
56	83	Scotsboro' and Jackson counties, "	May —, 1867		Chattanooga National Cemetery, Tenn.
57	99	Stevenson and Jackson counties, "	May —, 1867		
58	2	Big Shanty and Kenesaw Mount. Ga.	May —, 1867		
59	2	Between Brown's Ferry and Chickamauga, Tenn.	June —, 1867		
60	16	Vicinity of Stevenson, Ala.	July —, 1867		
61	10	Bellefonte, "	July —, 1867		
62	2	Thacker's Station, "	July —, 1867		
63	5	Mud Creek Bridge, "	July —, 1867		
64	8	Larkin's Landing, "	July —, 1867		
65	4	Claysville, "	July —, 1867		
66	2	Dotsonville, "	July —, 1867		
67	2	Woodville, "	July —, 1867		
68	9	Winchester road, "	July —, 1867		
69	1	Marshall, N. C.	July —, 1867		
70	7	Warm Springs, N. C.	July —, 1867		
71	1	Ashville, "	July —, 1867		
72	4	Parretsville, "	July —, 1867		
73	3	Paint Rock, "	July —, 1867		
74	1	Elliott's Ferry, "	July —, 1867		
75	3	Newport Ferry, "	July —, 1867		
76	1	Wilsonville, "	July —, 1867		
77	2	Grassy Fork, "	July —, 1867		

78	3	Dandridge and vicinity, Tenn	July, 1867		
79	3	Maysville and vicinity, "	July, 1867		
80	2	Fair Garden, "	July, 1867		
81	1	Seiverville, "	July, 1867		
82	1	Boyd's Ferry, "	July, 1867		
83	5	Knoxville, "	July, 1867		
84	10	Mission Ridge and vicinity, Tenn	Aug. to Nov., '67		
85	6	Near Stevenson, Ala	July, 1867		
86	8	Near Bridgeport, Ala	Aug. 1867		
87	2	Docktown, Tenn	Aug. 1867		
88	4	Road to Docktown, Tenn	Aug. 1867		
89	1	Silas' Creek, "	Aug. 1867		
90	9	Cleveland, "	Aug. 1867		
91	3	Trenton, Ga	Dec. 1867		
92	5	Sequatchie Valley	Oct. 1967		
93	1	Harrison	Oct. 1867		
94	3	Road to Summerville	Nov. 1867		
95	1	Bridgeport, Ala	Nov. 1867		
96	1	Decherd, Tenn	Nov. 1867		
97	2	Resaca, Ga	Feb. 1867		
98	29	Chattanooga, Tenn	Apr. to Dec. '67		
		Total removed to Chattanooga, Tenn		11,749	
1	3	Nashville, Tenn	From April —, 1868, to Aug. —, 1868.	543	Nashville National Cemetery, Tenn.
2	5	Nashville, "			
3	1	Lucas' farm, Tenn			
4	1	Dickerson Pike			
5	1	Edgefield			
6	312	Clarksville			
7	8	Elkin Bridge and vicinity			
8	3	Thomas Brown's farm			
9	4	Reynolds' Station and vicinity			
10	14	Buford's Station and vicinity			
11	13	Nashville and Columbia Pike			
12	76	Russellville, Ky			
13	102	Tompkinsville, Ky			
		Total removed to Nashville, Tenn		543	

IX.—From places in Indiana, Kentucky, and Virginia, to Indiana.

No.	Number of Graves.	NUMBER AND ORIGINAL LOCATION OF GRAVES. Original Location.	DATE OF REMOVAL OF BODIES.	FINAL DISPOSITION OF REMAINS. Number of Bodies.	Final Resting Place.
1	695	New Albany, Ind			
2	701	Jeffersonville, "			
3	526	Louisville, Ky			
4	108	Smithland, "			
5	24	Princeton, "			
6	28	New Haven, Ky			
7	41	I. McDougall's farm, Ky			
8	5	Buffalo Church Cemetery, Ky			
9	1	Hodgesville,			
10	136	Madison, Ind			
11	30	West Point, Ky			
12	1	Mrs. Young's farm, Ky			
13	32	Piketon			
14	5	Ivy Mount, Floyd county, Ky			
15	1	Hawe's Ford, "	From Ma 1866, to v 1. Aug.	2,788	New Albany National Cemetery, Ind.
16	4	Prestonburg, "			
17	1	I. H. Hareford's farm, "			
18	1	G. W. Auxire's farm, "			
19	1	I. Conley's farm, "			
20	22	Paintville, "			
21	2	Big Paint Creek, "			
22	5	Peach Orchard, "			
23	54	Louisa, "			
24	20	Thomas Wallace's land, "			
25	8	Judge Clayton's land, "			
26	4	Mr. Vincan's farm, "			
27	1	I. W. Hawe's farm, "			
28	7	Caletsburg, "			
29	2	Barborsville, Va			
30	5	Guyandott, "			
31	9	Cerdo			

32	171	Ashland, Boyd county, Ky.		
33	12	Maysville, "		
34	26	Flemingsburg, "		
35	75	Calhoun, "		
36	19	Madisonville, "		
37	3	Sacramento, "		
38	2	Rumsey, "		
		Total removed to New Albany, Indiana.	2,788	

X.—From places in Kentucky to Kentucky.

1	437	Covington, Ky.		
2	104	Frankfort, "	June and July, 1868.	
3	241	Richmond, "		2,023	Camp Nelson National Cemetery, Ky.
4	975	Perryville, "		
5	266	London, "		
		Total removed to Camp Nelson, Ky.	2,023	
1	341	Danville, Ky.		355	Danville National Cemetery, Ky.
2	14	Milledgeville, Ky.		
		Total removed to Danville, Ky.	355	

XI.—From Pennsylvania to Pennsylvania.

1	35	Braddock's Field Cemetery, Pa.	35	Alleghany Cemetery, Pittsburg, Pa.

XII.—From places in Illinois to Illinois.

1	73	Seven miles from Springfield, Illinois, near Clearlake, Ill.	Nov. —, 1868	73	Camp Butler National Cemetery, Ill.

ALPHABETICAL INDEX

TO

ORIGINAL PLACES OF BURIAL, WHENCE BODIES HAVE BEEN REMOVED.

Name of Locality.	Page.	Name of Locality.	Page.
Aquia Creek, Va	28	Cherrystone, Va	12
Amelia C. H., Va	13–15–16	Chickamauga, Tenn	33–34
Anderson, Tenn	33	City Point, Va	20
Appomattox C. H., Va	13–20	Clark county, Va	6
Ashville, N. C	34	Clarkville, Tenn	35
Athens, Tenn	33	Clarksville, Texas	30
Atlanta, Ga	33	Claysville, Ala	34
		Clearlake, Ill	37
Barborsville, Va	36	Cleveland, Ohio	31
Barrancas, Texas	30	Cleveland, Tenn	33–35
Bath county, Va	6	Cloud Spring, Tenn	33
Baton Rouge, La	31	Cold Harbor, Va	18
Battle Creek, Ala	33	Cortinas Ranch, Texas	30
Beaver Dam Station, Va	9	Covington, Ky	37
Belle Plain, Va	25	Craney Island, Va	12
Bellfonte, Ala	34	Crater	14
Bell Island, Va	18	Crawfords, Ga	32
Bermuda Hundred, Va	14–18	Cumberland Mount, Tenn	33
Big Paint Creek, Ky	36		
Big Shanty and Kenesaw Mt., Ga.	34	Dabney's Mill, Va	15
Blandford, Va	14	Dallas county, Mo	32
Bolivar, Mo	32	Dalton, Ga	33
Bolivar, Va	6	Dandridge, Tenn	35
Bottom's Bridge, Va	20	Danville, Ky	37
Bowers' Hill, Va	12	Danville, Va	21
Boyd county, Ky	37	Darksville, Va	6
Boyd's Ferry, Tenn	35	David's Cross-roads, Tenn	33
Braddock's Field, Pa	37	Decherd, Tenn	35
Brazos, Santiago, Texas	30	Dickerson's Pike	35
Bridgeport, Ala	32–33–35	Docktown, Tenn	35
Brook's Station, Va	28	Dotsonville, Ala	34
Brownsville, Texas	30	Dutch Gap, Va	15
Brûlé Creek, D. T	31		
Buffalo, Ky	36	Edinburg, Texas	30
Buford's Station	35	Edgefield	35
Bunker's Hill, Va	6	Elkin Bridge	35
Burgess' Mill, Va	14	Elk's Mills, Mo	32
Burksville Junction, Va	14	Elkton Heights, Va	6
		Elliott's Ferry, N. C	34
Calhoun, Ky	37	Ely's Ford, Va	24
Camback's Mill, Va	23		
Camp Hamilton, Va	12	Fair Oaks Station, Va	20
Caroline county, Va	30	Fair Garden, Tenn	35
Carpenters, Ala	33	Falmouth, Va	27
Cartersville, Va	19	Farmville, Va	15
Catlettsburg, Ky	36	Fayette Court-house, Va	22
Ceredo	36	Five Forks, Va	15
Chancellorsville, Va	23	Flemingsburg, Ky	37
Charles City, Va	12–19–20	Floyd county, Ky	36
Charleston, Tenn	33	Fort Damnation	15
Charlestown, W. Va	6	Fort Davis	15
Chattanooga, Tenn	32–34–35	Fort Gregg	15

Name of Locality.	Page.	Name of Locality.	Page.
Fort Harrison, Va.	19	London, Tenn.	33
Fort Haskins, Va.	16	Lookout Mount, Tenn.	32–34
Fort Hell, Va.	16	Loudon county, Va.	9
Fort Monroe, Va.	12	Louisa, Ky.	36
Fort Norfolk, Va.	12	Louisville, Ky.	36
Fort Steadman, Va.	17	Lovettsville, Va.	9
Frankfort, Ky.	37	Lurray Church, Va.	22
Franklin, Va.	21	Lynchburg, Va.	16
Frederick county, Va.	6–7–8		
Fredericksburg, Va.	24–26–27	McCool's farm.	23
Fredericks Hall Station, Va.	19	McDonald county, Mo.	32
Front Royal, Va.	8	Madison, Ind.	36
		Madison county, Tenn.	34
Gettie's Station, Va.	12	Madisonville, Ky.	37
Gordonsville, Va.	19	Marlboro' Point, Va.	28
Granville, Tenn.	33	Marietta, Ga.	31–33
Grassy Fork, N. C.	34	Marshall, N. C.	34
Gravelly Church, Va.	15	Martinsburg, Va.	9
Graysville, Ga.	33	Mary's Heights, Va.	27
Great Bridge.	12	Massaponax Court-house, Va.	23
Green county, Mo.	32	Massanuton Mount, Va.	9
Greenwood Mills, Va.	9	Maysville, Tenn.	35
Griffin's Spring.	19	Maysville, Ky.	37
Ground Squirrel Bridge.	19	Mead Station, Va.	16–20
Guyandott, Va.	36	Mechanicsville, Va.	19
		Milledgeville, Ky.	37
Halltown, Va.	9	Mine Run.	28
Hampton, Va.	12	Mission Ridge, Tenn.	32–35
Hancock Station, Va.	15–19	Moorefield, W. Va.	9
Hanover county, Va.	19	Monterey.	23
Hanson's Hill, Va.	9	Mountain Gap, Va.	9
Harper's Ferry, Va.	9	Mount Carmell, Va.	9
Harrisburg, Va.	21	Mount Gilead, Mo.	32
Harrison.	35	Mount Hebron, Va.	9
Harrison's Landing, Va.	15	Mount Jackson, Va.	9
Hatcher's Run, Va.	16	Mount Pleasant Landing, La.	31
Hawe's Ford, Ky.	36	Mud Creek Bridge, Ala.	34
Henrico county, Va.	19	Munley's Mill, Va.	19
Hodgensville, Ky.	36		
Hope Landing, Va.	28	Nashville, Tenn.	35
Hungry Station, Va.	19	Nazomi Church, Va.	16
Huntsville, Ala.	34	Naval Hospital, Va.	12
		New Albany, Ind.	36
Jackson county, Tenn.	34	New Haven, Ky.	36
Jackson's Mill, Va.	16	Newmarket, Va.	9
Jackson River Depot.	22	Newport News, Va.	12
Jackson's Sally Port, La.	31	Newport Ferry, N. C.	34
Jaspar, Tenn.	33	Newtown, Va.	9
Jamestown Island, Va.	12	Norfolk, Va.	12
Jeffersonville, Ind.	36		
Jettersville, Va.	16	Oak Grove, Va.	17
		Oakland, Va.	21
Kelly's Ferry, Tenn.	33	Ooltawah, Tenn.	33
Kingston, Tenn.	33		
Knoxville, Tenn.	35	Page county.	23
		Paint Rock, N. C.	34
Lacey's Spring.	22	Paintville, Ky.	36
Larkin's Landing, Ala.	34	Parretsville, N. C.	34
Laurel Hill, Va.	23	Peach Orchard.	36
Lee's Mill, Ga.	33	Perryville, Ky.	37
Liberty Church, Va.	16	Petersburg, Va.	15–17
Little Petersburg, Va.	9	Philadelphia, Tenn.	33
Locust Grove.	28	Piedmont, Va.	21
London, Ky.	37	Piketon.	36

Name of Locality.	Page.	Name of Locality.	Page.
Pine Hill, Va.	9	Smithland, Ky	36
Point Coupee, La	31	South Mills, Va	12–13
Point of Rocks, Va	20	Spottsylvania Court-house, Va.	25
Pole Green Church, Va	19	Springfield, Va	10
Polk county, Mo	32	Springfield, Ill	37
Pomme de Terre Creek	32	Stafford C. H., Va	28
Port Hudson, La	31	Staunton, Va	21
Port Republic, Va	21	Stevenson, Ala	33–34–35
Port Royal, Va.	29	Stevenson county, Tenn	34
Portsmouth, Va	12	Stony Creek, Va	17
Prestonburg, Ky	36	Strasburg, Va	10
Princeton, Ky	36	Stringer's Hill	33
		Suck Creek, Tenn	33
Raisher's Woods, Va	9	Suffolk, Va	13
Rancho Blancho, Texas	30	Summit Point, Va	10
Ream Station, Va	17	Sussex C. H., Va	17
Resaca, Ga	32–35	Sutherland Station, Va	17
Reynolds' Station	35	Sweet Run Swamp, Va	10
Rice Station, Va	17–18	Sweetwater, Ga	33
Richmond, Va.	18–19–20		
Richmond, Ky	37	Tantalon, Tenn	33
Ringold, Ga	32	Thackers Station, Ala	34
Rocketts, Va	19	Tompkinsville, Ky	35
Rocky Ford, Ga	33	Tracy City, Ga	33
Romney, Va	10	Trenton, Ga	35
Rose Hill Point	29	Tunnel Hill, Ga	33
Rossville, Ga	33		
Rumsey, Ky	37	Wade's Depot, Va	10
Russellville, Ky	35	Warm Springs, N. C	34
		Warren county, Va	10
Sacramento, Ky	37	Weaterly Chapel, Va	11
Safrona Church	17	Weid's Station, Va	11
Sailor's Creek	15–16	Wells Valley R. R., Ga.	33
Salem	23	Westmoreland Court-house, Va.	29
Santa Maria, Texas	30	West Point, Ky	36
Savage Station, Va	19	Whitehall, Va	13
Savannah, Ga	31	White Oak Swamp, Va	19–25
Sawyer's Lane, Va	12	Whiteside, Tenn	33
Seiverville, Tenn	35	White's Ranch, Texas	30
Senior Station, Tenn	33	White Sulphur Springs	22
Seven Pines, Va	20	Wilderness battle-field, Va	23–25
Sequatchie Valley	35	Williamsburg, Va	19
Scotsboro' county, Tenn	34	William's Island	33
Shell Mound, Tenn	33	Wilsonville, N. C	34
Shenandoah county, Va	10	Winchester, Ala	34
Sheppardstown, W. Va	10	Winchester, Va	11
Silas Creek, Tenn	35	Woodstock, Va	11
Sir John's Run, Va	9	Woodville, Ala	34
Smithfield, Va	12		

ALPHABETICAL INDEX

TO

NATIONAL CEMETERIES WHERE BODIES HAVE BEEN DEPOSITED.

	PAGE.		PAGE.
Baton Rouge, La	31	Marietta, Ga	31
Brownsville, Texas	30		
		Nashville, Tenn	35
Camp Butler, Ill	37	New Albany, Ind	36
Camp Nelson, Ky	37		
Chattanooga, Tenn	32	Petersburg, Va	13
City Point, Va	20	Pittsburg, Pa	37
Cleveland, Ohio	31	Port Hudson, La	31
Danville, Ky	37	Richmond, Va	18
Danville, Va	21		
		Savannah, Ga	31
Fort Dakota, D. T	31	Springfield, Mo	32
Fredericksburg, Va	23	Staunton, Va	21
Hampton, Va	12	Winchester, Va	6

www.ingramcontent.com/pod-product-compliance
Lightning Source LLC
Chambersburg PA
CBHW031449160426
43195CB00010BB/918